LIFE INSURANCE 101

LIFE INSURANCE 101

THE BASICS OF LIFE INSURANCE EXPLAINED

Written By

D.W. LINDSEY

Life Insurance 101
D.W. Lindsey

First Edition, 2023

TABLE OF CONTENTS

INTRODUCTION 1

CHAPTER ONE
THE PURPOSES OF LIFE INSURANCE 5

CHAPTER TWO
TERM INSURANCE 14

CHAPTER THREE
WHOLE LIFE INSURANCE 21

CHAPTER FOUR
UNIVERSAL LIFE INSURANCE 30

CHAPTER FIVE
ALL THE OTHERS 37

CHAPTER SIX
BUYING LIFE INSURANCE 50

CHAPTER SEVEN
HOW MUCH SHOULD YOU PAY? 59

CHAPTER EIGHT
LIFE INSURANCE PROVISIONS AND OPTIONS 71

CHAPTER NINE
BASICS OF COMMERCIAL INSURANCE........................89

CHAPTER TEN
BASIC PRINCIPLES OF LIFE INSURANCE.....................99

CHAPTER ELEVEN
BASICS OF DISABILITY INSURANCE..........................110

CHAPTER TWELVE
DISASTERS: INSURANCE ISSUES.................................119

CHAPTER THIRTEEN
CLIMATE CHANGE: INSURANCE PROBLEMS...........122

INTRODUCTION

Does the concept of life insurance give you a headache? Have you put off getting life insurance because you don't know how to get started? Are you unable to properly appreciate the life insurance plans you've bought or that someone else purchased for you? If you answered yes to any or all of these questions, this book can help you solve your life insurance troubles and may save you a large amount of money.

Here is a step-by-step procedure for estimating your life insurance requirements, finding a reputable provider, buying a policy, and reviewing your policy promptly each year. This eBook will help you take responsibility for your life insurance, understand it, and recognize any possible concerns before it is too late. This book is to assist individuals just beginning the process of shopping for life insurance, those who already have a policy, and those who are helping others make life insurance choices. If you're new to life insurance and don't yet have a policy, part I will walk you through the process of deciding how much and what sort of life insurance you need, and part II will help you select the best provider. Note that I'm presuming you certainly need life insurance. If you haven't decided yet, you may go to my website and utilize the "How Much Life Insurance Do I Need?"

If you're someone who already holds a policy and understands something about life insurance, part I serves as an ideal and important chance to complete a gap analysis: How well do both the policy you acquired some years ago and your life insurance company match your current needs? Your requirements may have altered alternatively you may not have done a full evaluation of your requirements when you originally acquired your policy, instead relying on your life insurance agents or financial adviser's recommendations. Part III will help you assess and evaluate your existing insurance and your choices. As with any other financial instrument, you must examine your life insurance policy yearly. If you no longer need coverage, I'll help you find out choices for ending your insurance. And if you are responsible for helping people analyze their life insurance requirements as part of an entire estate-planning or financial-planning strategy, this book may help you get to better answers quicker.

That is the objective of this book: to assist you in better using your life insurance funds to obtain the greatest price you can. Why pay more than you need to? A life insurance policy is, at the end of the day, an instrument for financial leverage—nothing more, nothing less. But this book is not about investing; it's about life insurance, and utilizing life insurance as life insurance.

If you want to invest your money to develop your nest egg or retirement assets, which by all means you should, seek elsewhere.

No matter what you read or hear, life insurance may act as a supplementary investment only when you have a life insurance need. It is not an investment instrument in and of itself since you will always have insurance payments on top of any other expenditures. Well, you may question, what about the fact that life insurance cash values build on a tax-deferred basis? First, this is not guaranteed. Congress frequently speaks of withdrawing this benefit of life insurance, and if it does, look out. Second, alternative tax-deferred vehicles are available, such as IRAs, 401(k)s, and others, Congress is not targeting taxes and those who do not have insurance payments. Unfortunately, many individuals are so preoccupied with profits that they disregard the significance of controlling their spending. It's the core of all smart financial budgeting: Any time you cut spending, your budget will improve.

So let's figure out the world of life insurance and how it fits into your overall plans.

CHAPTER ONE

THE PURPOSES OF LIFE INSURANCE

The number one reason to purchase life insurance is to protect your beneficiaries if you die early. That's apparent. Every other reason is secondary - but for certain individuals, the other objectives might take on more significance in specific circumstances.

Protecting beneficiaries

Protecting your survivors involves replacing the money you bring in the event you die early. If you have children, you presumably spend your wages on the expenses of bringing them up. If you die, your life insurance death benefit replaces those wages so that they won't have to suffer financially. If you have a mortgage on your property, a life insurance death benefit might assist your family remains in their home if you die. Life insurance may assist you to overcome the burden of having to fully alter your way of life because you lose half or more of your income.

Lastly, if you are part-owner of a corporation, the firm may get a life insurance policy on you so that if you die, your partner may use that death benefit to buy out your share of the business from your heirs.

Using life insurance as an investment

A second aim of getting life insurance is to utilize it as part of your investment portfolio. Most financial consultants recommend you balance your assets so that if one sort of investment goes down (the stock market, for example), another one will likely go up (bonds or real estate, maybe). By balancing your portfolio and diversifying your investments, you can weather storms in one area by having some assets in the other sectors that move up or remain level.

Some life insurance contracts are essentially long-term investments, which you may contribute to and take cash from before you die. These so-called cash-value plans whole life and universal life insurance are savings accounts that develop a cash value over time and also pay for your protection. Although these plans don't offer the best interest rates you can find, they are untaxed profits, so you receive a larger return than just putting your money in a savings account on which you must pay taxes.

Using life insurance as a tax shelter

Life insurance may serve two functions as a tax-sheltered investment:

- The profits on cash-value insurance are not taxed until you take them out.
- The profits of a death benefit settlement are not taxable to your survivors.

DECISION CHART

Evaluate Your Needs and Situation

Step 1: Determine your present need for life insurance: How much life insurance do you need? Or is your present life insurance enough?

Step 2: Determine what form of life insurance you need: Do you need term or permanent/whole life insurance? Or is your present coverage the correct kind to satisfy your current needs?

Step 3: Assess your medical history and other variables that might affect your life insurance premiums.

Evaluate Companies Agents and Purchase a Policy

Step 4: Evaluate life insurance companies and pick one with whom to collaborate.

Step 5: Choose an agency, consultant, or distributor.

Step 6: Work with your agent to determine the right insurance components and riders and buy a policy.

Understand, Maintain, and Monitor Your Policy or Terminate It

Step 7: Assess your policy to determine if it is living up to your expectations.

Step 8: Determine if replacing your coverage makes sense.

Step 9: If you no longer need your coverage or are opting to acquire a new policy, decide how to terminate/unwind the policy.

Calculating Your Need for Life Insurance

For some individuals, life insurance looks straightforward to grasp; nonetheless, it might be more difficult than anticipated at first sight. For others— especially those who don't know anything about it—it could appear exceedingly complicated. In truth, it's neither easy nor difficult, which is why the best route is to be a well-educated customer. And the best place to start is not with a discussion of life insurance alternatives but, instead, with a detailed look at your requirements. Answer the questions inside this step the best you can, but don't stress about getting everything completely, inflexibly "right." This exercise isn't about perfection—no one can predict the future for sure anyway. This is about ball parking it. It's about taking the best estimate. It's about contemplating where you are now, where you want to go, and where you want your loved ones to be in case the worst comes to occur. As Master Yoda would say: In motion the future is.

EXPLORING WHY YOU NEED LIFE INSURANCE

Following are several scenarios or life events that indicate a need for life insurance. Put a tick next to the descriptions below that best relate to your requirements for life insurance.

1. I'm a major earner for my family. I have small children and my family is entirely reliant on my income. If I were to die tomorrow, they would be in serious difficulty.

2. I've got debt. I have mortgages, vehicle loans, credit cards, college loans, or any other sort of massive, substantial debt that I couldn't bother my family or cosigners with if I died away tomorrow. It would break them.

3. I don't want to burden my family with the expenditures of my funeral.

4. I'm saving for my child's or children's private school or college education. If I departed away, the type of education that I'd want to be able to offer my kid or children might very well be out of reach.

5. I wish to have an emergency fund.

6. I have a special needs kid that relies on my income for his or her care, perhaps for the remainder of his or her life.

7. I'm concerned about estate taxes. I want my family to have liquidity at my death to finance the estate tax penalty.

8. I'd want to leave a considerable sum to charity after I die, but I don't necessarily want to considerably diminish the amount of my estate distributed to heirs.

9. I want to make sure my heirs each receive an equitable part of my assets when I die away.

10. I've got assets that haven't been taxed yet (a tax-deferred retirement account, for instance), and I don't want my family to be saddled with those taxes, or for those taxes to lessen the benefit my family gets upon my death.

11. I'm in a second or third (or beyond) marriage or domestic relationship, and I'd want to offer my new spouse financial stability; I want to prevent any disagreement that may develop concerning my inheritance after I die.

Looking at these situations, you can see that some are wider in context (the income-dependent ones) and others are much more specialized (like the treatment of inheritance taxes) (like the handling of estate taxes). Which scenarios best represent your circumstance will primarily rely on how much in assets you have or can reasonably anticipate having, what stage of life you're in, and your unique family status? Although these aren't exactly all the reasons for obtaining life insurance, they certainly reflect the most typical motives or reasons for acquiring it.

Use the area below to tailor your replies to the reasons you just picked. How do those possibilities relate especially to your situation? Or what requirement do you have that is not included here, and which previously indicated category would it most closely resemble?

DETERMINING HOW MUCH LIFE INSURANCE YOU NEED

Every consultant, financial writer, and relative has a formula they believe is optimal for estimating how much life insurance you need. Some of these formulas are simple, whereas others look like something only a Wall Street numbers wiz could dream up. But don't let complexity overwhelm or discourage you. If your demands are more complicated, a knowledgeable life insurance agent or financial consultant can help you calculate the proper amount for you. For most individuals, though, the simplest solutions are typically the best.

The greatest starting point for each of us in solving this equation is a basic, accurate grasp of our financial health. The more difficult we make things for ourselves, the greater the odds are that something won't turn out as intended. Life is lovely and lively. Ultimately, life insurance isn't about reducing something as valuable as life to numbers and statistics; it's about freeing us up to concentrate on what makes us happy.

Note that even if you may already hold a policy, it's still vital to do this activity. Why? Because your demands may have evolved as a consequence of various milestones in life, such as having children, children graduating from college, retiring, changing occupations, and so on.

For some individuals, this might be an emotional workout. Just try to be as realistic about your financial health as you possibly be. The correctness of every computation relies on the information utilized. The more assets outside of life insurance you have, the more flexible your projections about your life insurance requirements might be. The fewer assets you have, the more you'll need a realistic, practical prediction of your financial future. Don't get caught up on the minutiae you can't predict—again, this is about making the best guesses. Some of the questions in the worksheet may not apply to you.

Annuities

Most people conceive of life insurance as the major manner of safeguarding survivors or heirs. However, certain life insurance contracts, called annuities, give an income to the insured individual later on in life. Annuities are simply investment vehicles in which you dump down a boatload of money, either as a flat amount or in years of payments, in return for a guarantee from an insurance company that it would pay you a monthly income, generally after a predetermined time. Of course, that time won't occur until far after the corporation has earned enough money from you to make paying you financially sustainable for them.

Two kinds of annuities are available:

- **Fixed Annuities:** With a fixed annuity, the firm gives you a guaranteed rate of growth, depending on the amount you have paid in premiums and the conditions you have agreed upon beforehand. These payments might be either for a predetermined number of years or until you die.

- **Variable annuities:** With variable annuities, you may decide how and where the money is invested. The amount you're paid fluctuates based on how successful you and the company's investment money are.

You may tell the firm to invest in any combination of funds that the company provides — stock funds, bond funds, fixed-income funds, or other investment funds. Most insurance firms that sell annuities offer a reasonably broad choice of funds from which to pick, ranging from growth stock funds to global investment funds. Some have more risk, some lower.

As an investing potential, annuities aren't the best alternatives. You can normally perform better in other funds and with different accounts. However, with an annuity, you're investing and getting covered at the same time, which may be an attractive advantage for you.

Viatical Settlements

Life insurance includes a relatively new benefit called viatical settlements, which may alter your estate planning. With this scheme, terminally ill individuals may, in effect, "sell" the proneeds of their life insurance death benefit to a third party and obtain the cash they need while they're alive.

To qualify for this benefit, your doctor must certify that your life expectancy is no more than two years based on the fact that you have a terminal condition. The business then purchases your life insurance policy (including any cash value) for 60 percent of the face value. If your sickness has gone any further, and your physicians determine that you have fewer than six months, the viatical business will acquire your life insurance policy for up to 80 percent of the face value.

The purpose of the settlement is to ensure that terminally ill patients have the bulk of their life insurance benefits available to pay for their medical and living costs. On the other hand, terminally ill people must decide whether the life insurance benefits are for them or their survivors.

As you might think, this subject is quite contentious. You may discover more about this form of coverage by checking with an insurance firm that provides viatical settlements.

CHAPTER TWO

TERM INSURANCE

- Understanding term insurance
- Defining term insurance choices
- Looking into employee benefits
- Determining the advantages and downsides of term insurance
- Choosing a term insurance policy

Some believe that every sort of life insurance is term insurance: For all types of life insurance, you pay each year. The sole difference between term insurance and all the others is whether you pay the premiums directly (as with term life insurance) or the payment comes out of the returns from an investment that the insurance company keeps (as with other forms of life insurance) (as with other types of life insurance). In this chapter, I describe the qualities of term life insurance that separate it from the other versions.

I examine the many requirements that separate each characteristic and each form of term life insurance.

Understanding Term Insurance

Term insurance is the most basic kind of life insurance and, thus, the simplest to grasp. At its basic level, term insurance offers life insurance for a fixed time (typically a one-, five-, or ten-year term). For the insurance, you pay a monthly, quarterly, yearly, or semiannual premium that stays constant for a set time.

But that's pretty much the only constant. I can't even assume that the death benefit stays the same for the whole length of the coverage since numerous choices are available, such as decreasing term insurance and growing term insurance, in which the death benefit fluctuates each year (rarely more than 20 percent above or below the initial policy value). These two plans are distinct from level-term insurance, in which the death benefit stays the same for a predetermined time.

Term insurance offers a payout for others if you die within the stipulated time. Term insurance is not an investment - you get no rewards other than the peace of knowing that if you die, the insurance money go to your beneficiaries

Exploring Options in Term Insurance

Although term insurance is little more than a policy for a specified duration, it comes in many different forms, and you have many alternatives when picking a policy. The alternatives you must evaluate are outlined in the following sections.

Renewable term

The primary purpose of life insurance is so that your beneficiaries receive a benefit if you die. If you buy life insurance, not only do you want your policy to remain in effect during the specific period you designated, but you also want to be able to keep buying the insurance until you decide to stop not when the company decides that you've become too great a risk.

Most term-life policies are renewable but your premium may not be the same for the renewed period. After each term (the one-, five-, or ten-year period that you picked) expires, the amount you pay each year for the following term will climb.

A policy may be renewed only for a set duration (ten years, for example). So while looking for insurance, make careful to verify for how long it is renewed.

Without renewability, the insurance company might decide that it no longer wishes to cover you after the term of your policy expires. Renewable term insurance assures that you can still get life insurance regardless of the status of your health later; when you qualify the first time, you don't have to undergo any extra medical tests to keep your policy. And since you become a higher health risk as you age, not passing a medical exam is the hazard of not getting a renewable policy.

Renewable doesn't imply that you may adjust the face amount of your coverage. If you decide that you want extra insurance, the business will likely ask that you pass a new medical test to qualify.

Age Limitations

Many term insurance plans include an age restriction (defined in your contract) beyond which the firm won't allow you to renew your coverage. This age might vary from as low as 60 years old to 85, 90, or even beyond. Obviously, in the top age ranges most people have high risks, thus the price of coverage would be so expensive that it wouldn't cost for you to request coverage. But definitely, 60 or 70 isn't old, and many individuals at that age desire ongoing coverage.

When looking at term insurance products, make sure you pay regard to any age limitations set in the policy.

Convertible term

If you obtain convertible insurance, you are eligible to change to another form of policy – one that creates a cash value, such as whole life or universal life.

Most individuals don't continue to insure themselves once they reach retirement age, mainly because they no longer have anybody reliant upon them, but there are exceptions. For example, take a look at a family of four in which the father is 56, the mother is 43 and the two children are both under 10.

The younger kid won't attend college for another 15 years, and the parents want to make sure the children have adequate money even if the father dies. These parents may desire to maintain and ensure the father when he reaches the age of 70, the age at which his policy says that he may no longer renew his term insurance policy. To them, therefore, convertibility is a vital choice.

Another reason you may wish to be able to convert your term insurance is if your family has a history of heart disease, cancer, or another severe sickness. If your family history makes you more likely to get ill later in life, you may want to guarantee that you don't have to pass a medical test later, even after term insurance is not available. Because obtaining life insurance means, effectively, removing as much risk as possible, many individuals consider this provision an important one.

A third argument to preserve the convertible option has to do with the pricing of term insurance versus cash-value plans. Term plans often cost much less than other forms of life insurance since the others also create value while paying- ing for the policy. Convertibility may be crucial to you if you're on a tight budget but want cash-value policies. You know that you can convert later when you have better financial power.

Consider The Following Issues About Convertibility:

- To what can you convert your policy? Whole life? Universal life? Either one? Any product the firm provides later on?

- When can you convert? Some insurance stipulates how many years you have to convert. More time to decide provides you with more alternatives when you need them. Of course, the increased flexibility certainly implies a higher premium for the life of the term insurance.

- When you do decide to convert, would the new premium be dependent on your age when you convert? Or will the company require you to make a lump sum payment to "catch up," as though you had purchased the cash value policy, to begin with?

Decreasing term

For most term insurance policies, the death benefit remains constant and the premium increases over time. With a decreasing term life policy, the opposite is true: After the specified term, the face value of the policy decreases, while the amount you pay each year or month remains the same. In that way, the insurance company effectively increases its premium, which it must do because, as you age, you're at a greater risk for death. So the same premium purchases an increasingly lower amount of insurance.

For many people, decreasing term life insurance allows them to be insured to the maximum when they most need it (when their beneficiaries are most dependent on them) but to be insured for lower amounts as their beneficiaries need less. Because the premiums remain locked in, budgeting is simple you always pay the same amount.

Mortgage insurance is an example of decreasing term insurance. When you acquire mortgage insurance, you're making sure that your house mortgage is paid off if you die. But of course, while you're alive, you're paying off your mortgage principal, so the balance keeps declining.

Re-entry term

Renewable term insurance may have a provision called re-entry, which means that the insurance company can ask you to undergo a medical exam before it will renew your policy after the term expires. If your health isn't good and the re-entry clause permits it, the company can cancel your insurance. In return, you can purchase renewed insurance at a reduced rate — basically, the rate a person who just passed an exam would pay.

The gamble here is that you will remain healthy. Then then, if the re-entry provision doesn't let the firm cancel your insurance but does allow it to charge you higher rates, you're wagering on money, not your health. Some re-entry plans state forth the maximum premium that may be levied. If you're gambling, you ought to know how much you're gambling on.

When purchasing re-entry term insurance, make sure that you keep the right to renew your insurance even if you don't pass a medical exam. Although may have to pay higher premiums, at least the company won't be able to cancel your policy.

Employee benefits

Many organizations provide term life insurance coverage to their workers as a fringe perk. The sum generally varies from the equal of your yearly wage to treble your annual salary. The employer normally pays the whole premium.

Only the expense of the first $50,000 in life insurance is tax-free. Any premium an employer pays on your behalf for an insurance policy above $50,000 is extra income that you must declare on your tax return. In addition, this benefit is accessible to you only while you are working with the organization. When you depart, you lose the protection. If obtaining that insurance is part of your estate planning, you now have to reconsider your stance.

CHAPTER THREE

WHOLE LIFE INSURANCE

Whole life insurance insures you for your whole life, not just a short term. Your death benefit stays the same, and so does your premium. (With term insurance, your premium increases as you age to account for the fact that you're a bigger health risk.) Insurance companies keep both the premium and the death benefit constant during the life of a whole life policy by charging you a premium that's higher than the cost of the insurance when you're young and using some of that profit to pay for the higher cost of your insurance when you're older.

You may differentiate whole life insurance from term insurance in two major ways:

- You don't get insurance for just one year at a time with whole life insurance.
- You build up a cash value with full life insurance.

Compared to term insurance, therefore, you do seem to get more than you pay for with whole life. But that's not entirely true. In this chapter, I explain how cash value works and illustrate how the concept ties into whole life insurance policies. I also explain the many sorts of whole-life policies, the alternatives you have when acquiring a whole life policy, and the pluses and minuses of whole-life vs term insurance.

Cash Value

Building a cash value means that your life insurance policy has a value greater than just the death benefit — the face value of the insurance policy that goes to your beneficiaries when you die. (With term insurance, the value is only the amount of death benefit you sign up for.)

So what's the catch? Why would anyone want term insurance instead of a policy with a value beyond the death benefit? To address that question, you first need to study how cash-value whole life insurance works.

The investment concept

When you purchase a whole-life policy, a portion of your premium goes toward the life insurance itself, another portion goes toward your cash value, and the rest goes toward administrative costs and your agent's commission.

The insurance company invests the cash-value portion, and in return, you get some of the profits. Your portion goes towards your monetary worth. In a sense, then, this portion is an investment. Like all investments, it has its rewards.

Tax benefits

One of the biggest differences between this investment and many others is that all of the return on your investment is tax-deferred. You don't have to pay any taxes on this gain until you withdraw it, unlike other investments for which you must pay a capital gains tax. **An investment in whole life insurance becomes even more beneficial when you consider the following:**

- The part of your premiums that goes toward obtaining your actual insurance decreases the amount of gain you realize.
- You pay taxes only on the difference between the overall gain and the total premiums paid; making the return on your investment substantially better than if you had to pay taxes on the full item. (Even the capital gains tax is 20 percent, so if nothing else, you're collecting 20 percent more than if you placed this same money in an interest-bearing savings account.)

For example, if you obtain a 5 percent return on a savings account of $10,000, at the end of the year you have $500. But you also have to pay 20 percent of that return in income taxes. In effect, you only get $400 (20 percent of $500 is

$100, which, removed from $500, equals $400). In contrast, if the $10,000 is in a tax-deferred account, such as a whole life insurance policy, with an interest of 5 percent, you gain all of the $500.

If you're contemplating whole life insurance as a decent way to invest, bear in mind that the rate of return you earn historically has been pitifully low, even factoring the tax savings back in. Use the protection you're buying, not the rate of return you get, as your basis for judging any type of life insurance as an investment.

Rates of return

The rate of return you obtain from an investment in whole life insurance is reliant on the insurance company's ability to invest properly. The corporation aggregates all the cash-value money it receives from all its policyholders and invests this total, generally in low-risk assets, which naturally yield lower earnings than many other investments. Regardless of what return the firm obtains on its investment, however, most whole-life plans guarantee at least a minimum rate of return. Anything the corporation earns beyond that (and over and above its expenses) goes toward your cash worth.

The estimates that insurance brokers tell you are generally nothing more than great dreams, and you shouldn't depend on getting anything more than what is promised

If you look at the actual return, you can see that it's only a touch greater than the minimum guarantee. But it's also much lower than any of the more positive estimates the agent offered. Note that the cash value never surpasses the amount of the premiums paid with the 4 percent guaranteed return (which is barely above the minimum) (which is just over the minimum). On the other hand in part because of the original investment sometime around the 10th year, all of the premium paid goes toward the cash value, indicating that the interest on the reserve amount pays the cost of the insurance itself.

As you age, the cash value improves at a slower pace since your insurance costs more. From the 20th to the 25th year, for example, this insured pays over $4,000 in premiums, but his cash worth grows by just $1,200. That reduced return reflects the relatively high cost of acquiring insurance at age 60, suggesting that unless you still desire a death benefit at that age, you may choose to cash out the policy.

Dividends

Over and beyond the predetermined rate of return, some firms provide policyholders the option to profit from the company's success, just as shareholders do. The firm pays policyholders dividends, dependent on how well the company fared the previous year. Policies having this advantage are termed participation policies (commonly referred to as par plans in contrast to non-par policies that is, ones that don't pay dividends).

The amount of your dividend relies on a variety of factors:

- The company's overall financial success
- How well the firm predicted interest rates
- The number of claims the firm has to pay
- How successfully the corporation performed in its investments
- The particular terms of your insurance

Dividends are calculated into complicated calculations the outcome of which is your premium amount depends on the other alternatives the firm provides (such as loan perks), as well as the guaranteed rate of return.

Some firms offer a terminal dividend in a form of a bonus if you will follow the policyholder's death. Naturally, a corporation provides no warranty that it will pay this dividend (or any payout, for that matter), and you should consider that possibility while assessing competing programs. However, most yearly and terminal dividends are, indeed, paid.

When the insurance company announces that it will pay a dividend, it may pay the policyholder in cash, use the dividend to pay the cost of the acquired life insurance, put the money into the cash value, or use the amount toward new life insurance coverage. The selection is normally up to the policyholder, and there are reasons for selecting an either alternative. Naturally, the firm hopes you choose to use the cash toward more coverage most of the illustrations and examples that agents use in their sales presentations chose that choice.

The part of an annual dividend provided to you in cash that exceeds the premiums you paid for the year is taxable. A dividend paid to your cash value or used against your premium is not taxable until you remove monies from the account.

Traditional Whole Life

The following sections look at some of the particular elements of classic whole-life insurance.

Death benefit

With whole life, just like with term insurance, your heirs get just the death benefit the face value of the policy, meaning the protection you bought when you die, even if the premiums you paid also contributed toward a cash value. With whole life, none of the cash value you earn increases to the death benefit since the cash value goes toward paying the rising cost of the policy as you age.

Termination

If you cancel your whole life insurance, you're entitled to receive a surrender value, which is effectively the amount of your accumulated cash value. The surrender value continues to rise while you continue to pay to the insurance, but as you saw in Table 5-1, the amount increases at a gradually slower pace.

Policy loans

An additional advantage of whole-life plans is the fact that you may borrow against your cash value, generally at interest rates much lower than market rates between 6 and 8 percent.

The rates are so cheap because the lender is accepting virtually no risk if you don't pay back the loan, it may withdraw the money from your account. When you borrow against your policy, you don't have to pay any costs, and you may generally collect the money in only a few days. If you die before you pay back the loan, the outstanding amount is taken from the death benefit. If you discontinue the insurance, the outstanding loan amount is subtracted from the cash surrender value.

Interest-Sensitive Whole Life

Interest-sensitive whole-life insurance is a whole-life policy in which you are paid an adjustable, variable interest, rather than a guaranteed rate. Like an adjustable rate mortgage, the rate you are paid is sometimes connected to an economic indicator such as the Treasury Bill rate.

Premiums, death benefits, and cash value are all linked with the variable interest rate so that policyholders have multiple possibilities. When interest rates climb, you may keep the same death benefit and proportion that goes toward your cash value but cut your premiums. Or you may maintain the premium and death benefit unchanged while boosting your cash worth. In certain plans, you may boost your death benefit while keeping the premium and cash value rate of return unchanged.

Naturally, the opposite options are also available when interest rates are on the decline: cash-value returns decrease while premiums and death benefit are constant; premiums rise so that cash-value return and death benefit remain the same; or death benefits decrease while cash-value returns and premiums stay at the same levels.

Single-Premium Whole Life

Certain insurance firms provide single-premium whole life for clients who have a considerable quantity of money available to spend on insurance and who are seeking some tax advantages. You acquire the insurance by plunking down one big cash for a defined death benefit. You don't pay any yearly premiums, and the death benefit either stays constant or rises, depending on the sort of insurance you select. The insurance company takes your money up front, invests it, and provides you a tiny return, similar to what you receive with other whole life plans.

Like other whole life plans, a cash value does develop, generally with a guaranteed minimum return.

When the insured dies, the death benefit plus any accumulated cash value goes to the beneficiaries.

If you're sitting on extra cash and you want to acquire life insurance, consider this alternative. In effect, you pay all your premiums up front with single-premium whole life and then allow the firm to have use of your money for the whole duration. **In return, you receive a few perks that may be essential to you:**

- **You gain big savings on the cost of the insurance itself.** Your lump-sum payout is less than the total cost of yearly premiums on similar whole-life plans.

- **You earn large tax savings.** Tax savings may be the key reason many consumers obtain this sort of life insurance. All the money you earn on your single-premium whole life insurance is tax-deferred.

- **You may instantly borrow against the cash value in your account.** And if you just borrow against what the cash value itself earns, then you will likely pay nearly the same interest the cash value earns, as well. Thus, by holding some money in the company's coffers, you provide yourself the option to take out a loan nearly interest-free.

Don't acquire any form of insurance coverage solely on the rate of return or tax advantage you obtain. If you don't need or desire life insurance, you need to look into alternative, more lucrative means of saving money or minimizing your tax burden.

If you borrow against your whole life insurance policy, you need to pay special attention to the possible tax ramifications. If the amount you borrow includes any of the tax-deferred gain (the interest you've accumulated), you may have to pay taxes on the gain. Check with your tax expert before exercising this option.

CHAPTER FOUR

UNIVERSAL LIFE INSURANCE

Understanding universal life

- Learning about interest
- Borrowing against your cash worth
- Deciding on death benefits
- Determining premiums
- Determining the advantages and downsides of universal life insurance
- Choosing a universal life insurance policy

Universal life insurance gives freedom to policyholders. It's similar to whole life, in that you have a cash value that rises, and it incorporates a term life insurance, where you set the terms and renew the policy yearly. However, universal life isn't straightforward like term insurance or even like whole life. In reality, balancing the possibilities may be fairly hard. So in this chapter, I describe the principles of universal life insurance, the aspects that you get to compare for your requirements, and your possibilities in constructing the perfect policy for you.

- **How Universal Life Works**

  Universal life insurance is a sort of whole life insurance but with considerably wider flexibility. Like whole life, you have two components: a term insurance policy and an investment account from which the term insurance payments are paid. But with universal life, you get to select your possibilities, and the choices are typically put out in front of you. You know how the premiums may modify the death benefit and cash value, and it's more apparent how much of the premiums go toward your insurance protection, how much toward your cash value, and how much toward administrative expenditure (including commissions).

- **Start with a predetermined death benefit that you figure out with your agent.**
  You establish your anticipated premium, depending on how much you can pay and the cost of the insurance. The corporation subtracts a cost charge depending on its fees, usually a predetermined percentage of the premiums. You're left with a monetary value that earns interest.

- But understanding universal life insurance doesn't stop there. From the cash value, the corporation subtracts the current cost of insurance (the mortality charge), including the payments for any choices (or riders), and monthly administrative expenditures. Then the corporation puts the interest that your investment money generates. Your ending cash value is the cumulative wealth that belongs to you when you cash out (or to your beneficiary when you die) (or to your beneficiary when you die).

Often, corporations charge you a surrender price to cash out, leaving you with the surrender value. The surrender price is generally a modest fraction of the overall cash value.

Other elements of universal existence to explore include:

- All the profits in your investing account are tax-deferred.

- If you stop paying premiums, the firm continues to pay the premium for you by subtracting it from your policy's cash value. The corporation does so until no monetary value is left. This is one option to maintain coverage without paying premiums.

- The interest rate is a set rate, however, it may be a tiered interest rate, in which half is paid at one rate and the balance is paid at a higher rate. For example, your interest rate may be 4 percent for the first $500 and 7 percent for the balance.

- You may withdraw money that has been collected in your cash value. If you do, your death benefit lowers since it relies largely upon the accrued cash value.

- You may borrow against the cash value of your policy at a set rate, often below market rates.

- If you enhance your coverage, you may have to prequalify by completing a medical test.

- You probably have to pay a termination fee or surrender charge (backloading). This price lowers each year you keep the insurance, but it does lessen the amount of your cash value.

Generating Interest

Insurance firms usually have two or more interest rates that kick in at various levels. For example, the guaranteed interest rate may be 4 percent on the first $500 and 7 percent on balances exceeding $500. With a balance of approximately $8,000, the total interest is a little under 7 percent.

When you're picking a policy or firm from which to purchase your universal life insurance, choose the one with the greatest guaranteed interest so that your cash worth rises fast.

The interest earned continues to climb and ultimately will equal and then surpass the amount you invest. At this point, the money you pay is, in effect, flowing straight into your account.

The interest rate is determined daily, so you earn compounded interest (interest on your interest) (interest on your interest). For insurance with an interest rate of 7 percent, the annual percentage rate (APR) is more than 8 percent.

Borrowing Against Your Cash Value

Universal life plans let you borrow against your cash value, frequently at interest rates below what you can obtain elsewhere, even for loans secured against other assets. However, borrowing against your policy often decreases the interest you earn on your cash value, making it equal to or less than the rate at which you borrow.

For example, imagine that you get 4 percent on the first $500 of cash value and 7 percent on every amount over that $500. You now have an accumulated cash value, or surrender value, of $7,874. You may borrow $3,000 against this policy at a 6 percent interest rate — much below what you can obtain from a bank (even for another sort of secured loan) — so this bargain is extremely excellent if you need the cash. But the interest you get on the cash value of the insurance policy is no longer the 7 percent of the amount above $500. In reality, the interest you receive takes into account the $3,000 you borrowed, and the total interest you earn on your account is

- 4 percent on the first $500
- 6 percent on the next $3,000 (the amount borrowed) (the amount borrowed)
- 7 percent on the balance

Death Benefits Options

With universal life insurance, you can choose how much death benefit is to be paid. You have two possibilities, and while the options look comparable, certain tiny adjustments between them may affect the amount substantially. With both choices, your premium stays the same throughout the length of the policy, but the death benefit and surrender value change.

Option 1: Fixed death benefit

When you pick a set death benefit, whatever amount you sign up for (in the example, $50,000) goes to your survivors. In reality, the face value of the insurance the first $50,000 reduces by the amount you've collected in your cash value account. The death benefit stays the same since the lower face value and the increased cash value sum up to the entire amount you choose.

Option 2: Increasing death benefit

With the second option, your death benefit increases in line with the increase in your cash value. Your survivors get the surrender value, which certainly appears to be a great deal more for the consumer than Option 1 provides.

So what's the catch? Why would someone select Option 1? With Option 2, your cash worth improves more slowly than with Option 1. So you must continue paying the yearly premiums, frequently when you no longer require the same sort of protection you had 25 years ago.

Premiums

The quantities of your death benefit, accrued cash value, and premium are all connected with universal life. The more you spend every month in premiums, either the more protection you're purchasing or the greater financial value you're accumulating. You can't have both. The more protection you acquire, either the higher your premiums or the lower your cash value. And the more monetary value you want to generate, either the higher the premium or the less protection you're getting.

Because your main purpose in obtaining insurance is protection, your top consideration should be the size of the death benefit. Cash value and your premium cost should be secondary factors, but clearly, your premium should be in line with how much you can afford to pay.

Choosing your premium

If you desire universal life insurance and feel that you can pay the premium, you need to balance the following three elements to estimate your cash value:

- Determine how much you can spend from your monthly budget.
- Decide how much protection you want to purchase.
- Balance the amount of protection you want to purchase with the amount of premium you can afford.

You invest in a life insurance policy to be covered in case you die, not because life insurance is a good investment. You can generally make more money by putting your money into other investments.

Prepaying your premium

With universal life insurance, you can buy up-front by putting a significant sum into your account, which allows your cash value to increase more because your account is starting at a higher level. Prepaying also allows you to lower your premiums because the accumulated cash value is earned- in more, which means that more of your earnings can contribute to the cost of the insurance. On the other side, prepaying also implies that you must take a large amount of cash from someplace.

Is preparing for you? Not probable, unless you truly want insurance but can't afford monthly payments. People have traditionally utilized prepaid insurance as an investment to develop cash worth without suffering any tax repercussions. But with IRAs, Roth IRAs, and 401(k)s, odds are you won't be interested in this choice.

CHAPTER FIVE

ALL THE OTHERS

IN THE I S CHAPTER

- Looking for variable life insurance
- Understanding group life insurance
- Finding information about industrial life insurance
- Checking into mortgage insurance
- Exploring endowment life insurance
- Learning about various cyclists

In this chapter, I speak about an unusual variant of universal life, some of the many choices you have with all insurance, and several ways you may save money by combining with other individuals. I also discuss riders, which are some of the choices you may acquire.

Variable Life

A variant on whole and universal life insurance (see Chapters 5 and 6, respectively) is a variable life insurance policy. Under the terms of this form of insurance, you maintain a cash value from which your term insurance premiums are paid. What makes this type of policy different is that the cash value is invested in mutual funds. The amount of your death benefit is connected to the mutual fund's performance.

Variable life investments

Typically, you have the option of putting your cash worth in a common stock mutual fund, a bond fund, a money market fund, or any mix of funds. You keep control. With certain variable life insurance contracts, you may change funds, but you're constantly investing in the insurance company's funds. The profitability of these funds relies on how good the insurance company's investment managers are.

Variable life-death benefits

The amount of your death benefit with a variable life insurance changes but is often never below the face value. If your investments go higher, so does your death benefit. If it decreases well, so does your death benefit. That's one of the main perils of this sort of strategy.

If your investments go down, so, too, does your death benefit! And remember, you're buying life insurance, not as an investment but to protect your survivors if you die. Consequently, some insurance professionals are wary of this type of insurance.

However, a variable life policy with a minimum guaranteed death benefit is a whole different story, at least as far as protection goes. With a guaranteed death benefit, variable life can be excellent insurance policies because if the investments are successful, the cash value can go up much more than a policy with a fixed rate of return.

Straight versus universal variable life

You can get two different kinds of variable life policies: a straight variable policy, in which your premium is fixed and the death benefit rises and falls as the investments go up and down, and a variable universal policy, in which the premiums vary, the death benefit is either fixed or increases (just like a normal universal life policy), and your cash value goes up and down with your investments.

With the straight variable, if the value of your investment surpasses a set minimum (typically 4 percent), the death benefit increases boosted by that amount. If your investment's value declines, so does your death benefit. And with most policies, your death benefit will never decrease below the original face value.

If you're contemplating getting a straight variable life insurance policy, check certain it offers a guaranteed death benefit.

Other expressions of variable life

Most of the other terms of variable life insurance are the same as a universal life policy:

- You may borrow against your cash worth.
  In many plans, the amount you borrow is restricted by the amount that's put in a money market fund, which frequently receives a lower rate of return than stock or bond funds. This sort of defeats the purpose of buying this kind of policy to take advantage of the more dramatic rises in the stock market.
- You may opt to have an increasing or fixed death benefit.
- Your cash-value profits are completely tax-deferred, which provides value for many individuals.

The bottom line on variable life

For many people, variable life is an excellent product because it combines flexibility and bigger returns. But it also puts in much greater prices. The premiums are substantially greater than universal life, in part because the expenditure charges are much higher. Remember, your investments are paying not just for the cost of your term life insurance but also for the cost of the company's investment managers.

The purpose of life insurance is to protect your survivors. Although you want to choose the right kind of policy for your needs, you're not insuring yourself to make a killing on the market. So make sure that any policy you buy, especially a variable life policy, has a guaranteed death benefit. If you're searching for a solid return on your money and want to invest, especially in a tax-deferred vehicle, you're usually better suited to doing so via an IRA or 401 (k).

Group Life

Life insurance, like every other commodity, is cheaper when you purchase a lot of it (which is why $100,000 plans aren't treble the price of $50,000 policies), and cheaper when a lot more people buy it. When tens, hundreds, or thousands of individuals agree to purchase insurance from one firm, that company may offer prices substantially cheaper than if you buy a policy on your own.

Typically, group life insurance is acquired via your company or an organization to which you belong. One of the main things to remember regarding group life policies is that you don't own the policy! Although you're the one who is insured, the insurance belongs to your company or organization, not you. If you find a new job, retire, or resign, or you no longer are a member of the organization through which you acquired the insurance, you can no longer get the coverage.

Be aware that you may face tax repercussions when your company pays for your life insurance. The premium that your company pays for your life insurance coverage is, in fact, income. Therefore, you're responsible for paying taxes on that income. However, under the current tax rules, employers are allowed to provide up to $50,000 in term life insurance for you without your facing any tax consequences. Any premium paid for a policy above that minimum is considered additional income for which you must pay taxes. So if your employer purchases a $250,000 term life insurance policy for you, for which the company pays $850 per year (and the company can buy a $50,000 policy for $300), you must count the additional $550 as income on your tax return.

The cost of group term life insurance above $50,000 is item C in Box 13 of your yearly W-2 Earnings Summary.

Industrial Life

Industrial life often termed burying life, is a particular sort of insurance that isn't that prevalent. As its name implies, the policy pays a small amount to your beneficiaries for your burial expenses. The premiums are quite low because the policy's face value and the cost of burial are fairly low. In essence, industrial life is another term for life policy, but the death benefit is specifically tied to the cost of burial.

For most people, industrial/burial life insurance is not a good buy. It's usually more expensive than simple term insurance and doesn't pay your beneficiaries for anything other than your burial. If, however, you feel that you would like enough coverage to pay for your burial, you should speak with an agent about buying or increasing a life insurance policy.

Mortgage Insurance

Mortgage insurance is, essentially, another term insurance program designed specifically to pay the balance of your home mortgage. As you pay off your mortgage, the balance declines, and so does your mortgage insurance death benefit.

Endowment Policies

Endowment insurance policies are unique because they're both savings plans that build cash value and term life insurance policies that expire if you don't die. People who want the proceeds of their insurance to go to some organization, such as a college or charity, may take out endowment policies.

Riders

Riders is the term used in the insurance business for options that you can purchase as extras. Riders are some of the most important parts of the policy. When you purchase a life insurance policy, pay special attention to the riders being offered.

Most riders cost you additional fees. But one, an automatic premium loan, is almost always offered to you at no charge if you have a cash-value policy (whole life or universal life) and you check off the box that requests it. With this rider, the company pays your premium from your cash value if you don't pay, either because you forget or because the payment is never received.

For most insurance policyholders, taking this rider is a smart decision. Remember, insurance is protection. Don't get caught without protection just because your check gets lost in the mail or you forget to send it in.

Family rider protection

One of the options available with cash-value policies whole life, universal life, and most variable life is the opportunity to purchase a term life insurance policy for others in your family under your cash-value policy. This benefit usually saves you a great deal of money.

Say, for example, that you're 40 years old and you buy a universal life or whole life policy. You're building some cash value and, at the same time, using your premium to buy your term life coverage and add to your cash value. As the cash value grows and earns interest, either more of your premium goes toward your cash value, or the additional amount it earns goes toward paying the higher premiums for your coverage.

You may also want to cover your spouse in the event of his or her untimely death because both of you bring in income to support the family. If you go out and buy a separate term life policy for your spouse, you're probably going to pay much more than if you broaden your coverage to include the other person.

Double indemnity

Double indemnity is also called accidental death. Essentially, this rider pays your survivors twice the amount of the policy if you die an accidental death, as opposed to death by disease or illness. Some policies offer a triple death benefit if the accident occurs while you're a passenger on a common carrier, such as a commercial airline, train, or bus.

Accidental death riders sometimes raise questions about whether a death is a result of an accident or illness or disease. Most policies specify that to be covered under this rider, the insured must die within 90 days of an accident, and the cause of death must be directly related to the accident and that may be hard to prove.

Although accidental death/double indemnity riders are quite cheap, for most people they're not good deals. After all, you base how much you insure yourself for on your survivors' needs, and an accidental death won't increase the amount they need. (In fact, they probably need less than if you die from an illness because illness often brings additional and prolonged costs.)

If this coverage appeals to you, you probably feel underinsured. Instead, consider raising your amount of coverage.

Nondeath and living needs benefits

Another rider advantage that many plans (especially newer ones) provide is a non-death benefit when the policyholder gets the insurance payment without dying.

One of these sections covers accidental dismemberment, in which you lose an arm, a leg, or eyesight in one or both eyes owing to an accident (not a sickness or disease) (not an illness or disease). Typically, you may get a fraction of the complete face value, depending on whether you lose one limb or two, one eye or two, and so on. The insurance policy explicitly specifies the sums you get in each scenario.

You can also get a policy rider to cover you if you suffer a catastrophic illness such as a stroke or kidney disease, and a rider if you suffer from a terminally ill disease. This kind of coverage has become increasingly popular as more and more people face the issues of aging, AIDS, and high-tech medical care that extends lives.

With this rider, if you are terminally ill and have less than one year to live (your physicians must produce certified declarations to that effect), your insurance company will enable you to, in effect, take an advance on the face value of your death benefit. Usually, you may remove a portion of the whole coverage potentially as much as half, but more usually one-quarter or one-third. Most companies charge a fee to make use of this benefit, the amount of which varies on how much coverage you have and the proportion you're withdrawing. The amount you take out reduces your death benefit, so if you live longer than expected, your coverage is lower.

Don't mix this form of coverage with disability insurance, which covers your expenditures if you become partly or fully handicapped and can't work, or long-term care insurance, which pays for nursing home care or in-home nursing care.

This coverage is a real payout from your life insurance company because you're terminally sick and you want to be able to spend part of the death benefit before you die.

Cost of living adjustments

Another rider that many people feel passionate about is the cost of the living rider. It works very simply: Each year, the amount of death benefit rises depending on some impartial statistic, generally the Consumer Price Index (CPI) published by the federal government. If you choose this rider, the face value of your insurance policy automatically increases by this percentage. **For example:**

If you have a $100,000 policy and the CPI is 3 percent, the coverage goes up 3 percent, to $103,000.

The next year, when the CPI is 2.5 percent, your coverage rises 2.5 percent, to $105,575.

Naturally, you don't get this additional benefit for free. Instead, either your premiums increase to pay for the extra coverage or, if you have a cash-value policy and your premium is constant, the insurance company decreases the amount that goes into your cash value.

One of the perks of a cost-of-living rider is that your coverage gets boosted without your having to re-qualify for a higher amount. That means no new medical tests later in life when you may not qualify.

In that regard, this rider can be a pretty good deal: Your insurance coverage goes up to reflect the new needs of your survivors without your having to worry that you won't qualify for the higher amount.

On the other hand, the amount of increased coverage can be pretty small. In the last several years, for example, the inflation rate has been quite low. Adding 2 or 3 percent is not going to make any difference to your survivors. Secondly, with most plans, you get to pick each year whether to buy the larger amount. But if you refuse in any one year, you no longer have the choice in coming years and have to re-qualify if you wish to acquire the rider again.

If this rider appeals to you, chances are your worry is truly more about the overall protection you have acquired than the tiny annual increments. Speak with your family, your financial adviser, and your insurance agent about these issues. And if any event happens in your life that merits expanding your coverage the birth of a kid or a new job that results in a substantial rise in the expense of your living, for example, acquiring a bigger policy.

Guaranteed insurability

The thought that you can always get extra insurance later if you need to is quite alluring to individuals, making the guaranteed insurability rider seem intriguing. With this rider, you purchase just what you need today, and when your circumstance changes later on and you need or desire extra protection, you merely buy more. You don't have to worry about re-qualifying; you simply buy a new amount at the current standard rates for someone your age.

For the privilege of being able to buy more insurance later without having to re-qualify, you pay more now. And with most guaranteed insurability riders, you can exercise this option only until you're 45 or 50 years old (or a defined period of years, depending on the terms of your policy), which means that the additional payments you make along the way are wasted if you don't increase your coverage by then. Furthermore, this rider is only offered with cash-value policies, which already cost more.

If you decide to acquire that further security, be sure that you know how long you have to exercise your choice.

Policy protection: Waiver of premium

If you become handicapped and can no longer work, you probably won't be able to pay your life insurance payment either.

By purchasing a waiver of premium rider, you ensure that your insurance isn't canceled, even though you don't pay the premiums. You usually have to wait six months from the time you become disabled before this benefit kicks in.

Read the definitions and terms in these riders carefully and discuss them with your agent. Some waivers take over the payments if you can't work in your chosen profession (or a profession in which you have experience or for which you're trained), while other waivers of premium riders pay only if you can't work in any job. Still, others may combine these conditions such that for some time (two years, for example), the employer waives the premium if you can't work in your typical area of work, but after that waives the premium only if you can't work in any employment. The insurance company wills most likely conduct its medical exam to verify that you are disabled and unable to work.

For universal life insurance customers, the waiver of premium riders works a little differently. Because a changing portion of your premium goes toward the insurance coverage and the rest for administrative fees and cash value, the waiver of premium rider only covers the cost of the insurance and the administrative fees. No increases are made to your cash-value part save from any interest that is generated.

Buying this rider normally costs you 5 to 10 percent extra, maybe greater for term life since you're continuously renewing it. To qualify, you must have evidence from your physician showing you've been incapacitated and can't work.

For most life insurance holders, a waiver of premium rider is probably not such a good deal. You're better off increasing a disability insurance policy because it would pay for your expenses including a life insurance premium if you become disabled. But if you don't have disability insurance, this rider may be an inexpensive means to add that coverage without having to buy a whole new disability policy.

CHAPTER SIX

BUYING LIFE INSURANCE

After you find out about the many insurance products available, you need to start thinking about which product to buy and which firm to acquire it from. In this chapter, I lead you through the process of appraising a firm by the ratings, picking an agent, and selecting the proper product. I also explain about qualifying for life insurance, with specific attention on the medical test and what to do if you're not in excellent health, you smoke, or you work in a high-risk profession.

You have two guidelines to follow when purchasing a life insurance policy:

Rule 1: Choose the firm, not the agent.

Rule 2: Choose the insurance product, not simply the provider.

Selecting the Right Company
As with any product you buy, keep the following points in mind throughout your search for a life insurance provider:

- ✓ Make sure that you're picking the proper firm for your requirements.

- ✓ Be assured that if you're unsatisfied, you may cancel your insurance without paying any costs.
- ✓ Make sure that the insurance firm backs up its product, even if an individual agent goes out of business.

Insurance is a unique commodity. You're purchasing the future, not the present. You have to get the greatest goods from a firm you know can deliver when called upon. The entire objective of insurance is protection for your survivors. The product doesn't even come into existence until you die. So when you're picking a firm from whom to acquire the goods, do everything you can to be certain the company will be there to pay off.

Checking into a company's ratings

Five main independent insurance rating firms examine practically all the insurance companies (you can find their contact information in the Resource Center at the back of this book):

- ❖ A.M. Best Company
- ❖ Duff & Phelps Credit Rating Co.
- ❖ Moody's Investors Service
- ❖ Standard & Poor's Insurance Rating Services
- ❖ Weiss Research

Each of these rating services has its strong and poor qualities, and the ratings are not all constant. **But they all do roughly the same thing:**

- ➢ Analyze the financial soundness of insurance firms
- ➢ Evaluate the stability of insurance firms
- ➢ Make judgments on the credibility of insurance firms

Most pros believe strongly that you should not get a life insurance policy from a firm before you check out its rating.

When picking an insurance provider, check the ratings on many from at least two rating firms. The rating systems vary: An A from Weiss, for example, is the second-best rating a firm can obtain. Only an A+ is better. But an A from Standard & Poor's is far further down the list. It's sixth, after AAA, AA+, AA, AA-, and A+. Quite a change.

Even if you can equal the scales, the ratings of the rating agencies vary from one another. For example, Best may provide an insurance firm it's a top rating (AAA), while Moody's offers the company its fourth-highest rating (Aa3). So how can you judge?

What if the firm goes belly-up?

If a firm does collapse, odds are excellent that your protection will be fulfilled. The insurance regulators (state and federal authorities) cooperate with other firms to take up the policies of a failing company. If that attempt fails, your policy may be taken up by a guaranty association, a state organization made up of all the insurers in your state who jointly promise that you won't be left in the lurch.

Although these backups are reassuring, if your state association takes up your policy because no other insurance provider would, you may lose some of your benefits. Most state guaranty organizations have restrictions on the death benefit (usually not more than $500,000), and they also may not match the interest you're guaranteed on cash-value insurance. Check with your state insurance commission for additional information regarding insurance business bankruptcy.

The greatest thing you can do to make sure you don't lose your money or your protection is to pick your life insurance provider properly.

Selecting the Right Agent

Many insurance "stores" carry a variety of different "brands" of insurance. These sorts of insurance businesses or sales agents serve as independent brokers, bringing you, the consumer, together with the insurance provider.

In this instance, you pick the agent before you choose the insurance provider. This strategy appears to go against Rule 1, but in fact, you haven't yet picked the firm. You've picked an agent to offer you alternatives. Hopefully, the agent will show you items from more than one firm, enabling you to pick both the correct product and the right company.

If the agent can provide you with just one firm, reassess your stance and consider the first rule: **Choose the company, not the agent.**

Many insurance agents conceive of themselves as counselors as well as sales professionals. They have a selection of things to offer, one of which you're interested in purchasing. The agent's responsibility is to assist you to determine which one.

Your insurance sales representative is a qualified resource for you who may act as a counselor, helping you select which policy is best for you. Therefore, you need to locate someone you trust. Through open communication, your agent should be able to direct you to the proper product.

Beware of high-pressure techniques. Although most sales agents are honest, you may stumble into a slick, hard-sell insurance salesman who merely wants to sell you anything without appropriate care for your requirements or your budget. Check with others who use a potential agent, and make sure that he or she is a registered member of the National Association of Life Underwriters (NALU) or the Society of Financial Service Professionals.

Shopping for Insurance Online

As more and more items become accessible over the Internet, more and more individuals are buying insurance online. Hundreds, or maybe thousands, of Web sites, are dedicated to insurance, with more cropping up every day. At the time of this writing, a search for "life insurance," using one of the main search engines (www.excite.com) produced hundreds of hits. An examination of only 10 of these matches, picked practically at random, indicated that the majority may lead you to a firm from whom you can purchase life insurance.

Buying via the Mail

Most experts frown on obtaining life insurance from a direct-mail flier sent out to you and thousands of your closest friends offering you personal care. Although purchasing a life insurance policy over the mail may have been a great choice a few years ago, now it pales when compared to the pros of buying online.

But if a flier grabs your curiosity, consider it just as much as you would an insurance policy you find via an internet search. Do your homework. Compare terms, pricing, and business ratings, and chat with a trustworthy agent (or a suggested agent) to discover whether the firm is authentic. Make sure that you can speak with someone at the firm itself.

Qualifying for the Coverage You Want

The principle of life insurance is simple: Although you hope you live a long life, you also pay a business to make sure that if you die sooner rather than later, your survivors have something to fall back on. The corporation, similarly, is hoping that you don't die before it has a chance to profit more from what you pay than the expense of supporting your survivors. You know that you will die someday the only issue is when. Your only gamble is which insurance provider you select.

But firms don't want to risks, so they stack the deck. The more likely you are to die sooner than later, the more the firm wants to obtain from you in the early years of your insurance. If, on the other hand, the firm can bank on you staying around for a long time, it doesn't need as much each month to generate a profit off your premiums.

So how does the corporation make this judgment? **It utilizes the responses to two questions:**

- ✓ Based on sophisticated statistical studies and lifespan charts, how long are you expected to live?
- ✓ Based on your medical history and facts, are you a high or low risk?

The firm then bases your rates on the responses to those questions. If you're too old or too unwell, the business doesn't want to insure you since it will probably have to pay off before it can make a profit from your premiums (or it'll charge you so much that the cost won't be worth the coverage to you).

To qualify for a life insurance policy, you have to pass two conditions: You have to be young enough, and you have to be healthy enough.

The aging condition is based primarily on information acquired from huge numbers of individuals. If you're older than 60 or 65, most firms won't cover you. If you're younger than that, the firm will cover you, based your rates on your age.

To determine your medical condition, the firm will require you to supply your entire medical history and, for most plans, will ask you to undertake a medical exam.

Taking the medical exam

Medical exams for life insurance can involve anything from a quick review of your medical history, and your family's medical history, noting your height and weight and taking basic vital signs (blood pressure and pulse) and a swab of cells from the inside of your cheek, or it can be a more extensive exam requiring an EKG (electrocardiogram), blood tests, X-rays, and urinalysis. In addition, on your insurance application, you grant the insurance provider authority to verify with your doctor to follow up on any discoveries or dubious things on the application.

The scope of your physical exam is dependent on the following:

- ❖ Your age
- ❖ Your medical history
- ❖ Your family's medical history
- ❖ Whether you smoke
- ❖ The quantity of insurance you're trying to acquire

For rapid evaluation, normally a health expert comes to your house or business. If you need to undertake extra testing, the corporation may require you to visit a physician or travel to a clinic. The insurance company covers the expense of the test (although, of course, such administrative fees are factored into the cost of the insurance policy you buy) (although, of course, such administrative costs are built into the cost of the insurance policy you purchase).

What "high risk" implies

Insurance companies are worried about a variety of high-risk people:

- Smokers
- People with high cholesterol
- Potential diabetics
- People with indicators of coronary disease
- People having a personal history of cancer or other severe illness
- People who work in high-risk jobs

If you fall into one or more of these categories, you face three potential outcomes:

- The Company won't insure you.
- The Company will charge you a greater premium.
- The Company will overlook the high danger (which isn't probable).

What if I fail the exam?

If the firm refuses to cover you because of your medical condition, first ensure that the medical report is true. Request that the corporation gives a copy either to you (which they may not do) or to your doctor (which they will do). Go through the report with your doctor. You may be suffering real health problems that you need to address.

If you uncover a mistake in your medical report, tell the insurance company in writing immediately. Being turned down for life insurance might affect other insurance applications that you may be completing.

If the medical report is true and the firm charges you a greater premium, appeal to the agent who sold you the policy, but chances are you'll have very little success altering the amount. You may switch to a new firm, but they're likely to uncover the same faults and hike their premium as well. At that moment, you either pay the greater premium or drop the face value to lower the premium. You might also attempt to discover an insurance policy that doesn't need a medical exam or that requires just a short exam. (An independent agent may be able to direct you to another firm.) In any event, address the problem with your agent to see if the two of you can come up with a solution.

CHAPTER SEVEN

HOW MUCH SHOULD YOU PAY?

IN THE I S CHAPTER

- Calculating premiums
- Dealing with mortality charges
- Understanding underwriting
- Comparing rates and businesses

Insurance companies employ formulae to estimate how much danger you pose and measure that against how much profit they can earn. This chapter demonstrates how insurance companies calculate their premiums, informs you about the elements that determine your rate and points out some of the hidden costs you need to know about. The chapter closes by discussing the fundamentals of how to compare one company's policy with another's.

How Premiums Are Calculated

Before you can assess if a premium is affordable, you have to know how insurance companies compute the cost. So many of the expenses are concealed within the cash value, expected profits, and dividends that finding out how much you're spending isn't as straightforward as it seems, even with term insurance. You know how much goes out of your bank account each month for the insurance. And you know at the end of each year how much the surrender value is, assuming you have cash-value insurance. Theoretically, you can merely subdivide the amount in your account from the amount you paid out. But what about next year? What about cancellation charges? The next sections take you through the basics.

The expenses of term insurance

Every year (or every month or quarter or semiannually), you pay a specific premium for term insurance, which protects you for that time. In the following period, you pay again, either the same amount or a larger amount. Whether the sum is larger depends on whether you purchase a one-year term, a five-year term, or another multiple-year policy.

If you have one-year term insurance, you pay the one year and the firm boosts the premium each year. You don't know how much you'll pay next year. With one-year term coverage, you don't know how much you'll pay three or four years from now. Most firms can offer you a very decent estimate (provided that you select a company that has a proven track record of estimating accurately). But the question is if the firm produces dividends. If your premium is $346 per year and the dividend is $183, you pay only $163. If you buy a five-year term policy, the company declares the $183 dividend for all five years and you pay the same $163 each year. If you want to renew for another five years, you pay the next premium less the dividend rate for five more years.

The expenses of cash-value insurance

Term insurance is straightforward. Cash value, as you may have suspected, isn't that straightforward. Cash value is also significantly more costly since you're paying not only for the protection, administrative fees, and commissions, but also to build up the investment so that the income it earns will cover the expenses of the insurance, fees, and commissions. In addition, you're paying extra for the freedom cash-value insurance affords you.

The one thing that's easy about cash-value plans is that the premium stays the same for the whole duration.

So what changes? Well, everything else, including, in many situations, the amount that goes to your survivors.

When you acquire a cash-value policy, you pay a specific premium depending on the level of protection you're getting; the amount required to cover the insurance company's other expenses and the guaranteed amount that will accumulate in your account. How all those figures are structured is an extraordinarily intricate process based on amortization tables, actuarial mortality charts, and contracts with life insurance salesmen.

Unless you have a burning desire to wade through the numbers, the only things you have to be concerned with are

- How much protection you're purchasing (so that the death benefit is adequate for your requirements) (so that the death benefit is sufficient for your needs)

- The amount of your total premium (to make sure that you can afford the monthly payment) (to be sure that you can afford the monthly payment)

- The guaranteed return (so you know how much will go into your investment) (so you know how much will go into your investment)

Mortality Charges

When you take things down to the base fundamentals, life insurance is about how much you have to spend to cover your loved ones. **The insurance company decides your rate as follows:**

1. The insurance company and the industry at large keep statistics on the mortality rates throughout the country, based on its research or by relying on research done by others, such as the National Association of Insurance Commissioners. Through this research, the insurance company knows how many men and women in various age ranges (for example, 25- to 29-year-olds, 30- to 34- year-olds, 35- to 39-year-olds, and so on) die each year.

2. The insurance company uses these figures and several others to assess your life expectancy.

3. The insurance company then calculates how much money it has to make on your premiums so that when it pays your survivors, it pays less than what it has earned.

   Does it imply that if you had a $50,000 death benefit you will have paid more than $50,000? No. Not. In reality, odds are with term insurance you'll have spent little more than half to two-thirds of that number, depending on your age when you die. Keep in mind that the insurance company earns money on the rates you pay. Many other policyholders continue to pay premiums, and the firm utilizes these premiums to pay out death benefits. Many individuals pay payments for years but quit their insurance before they die, and the company gets to retain all that money.

4. The insurance company builds in the commission it pays the salesperson who sold you the policy.

5. The insurance firm adds in the additional expenses of conducting business, such as overhead, administrative costs, wages, employee perks, and profit. Even mail-order or internet policies require certain expenses for conducting business.

6. The insurance company totals all these values, which is the mortality fee.

Underwriting

Underwriting is the process by which the insurance company assesses whether or not it will cover you is the very core of insurance. And if you're declared insurable, underwriting is the process through which they assess how much to charge you for the protection.

When establishing whether or not you're insurable and what your premium will be, the insurance company puts you into one of three categories of risk, but you do have some freedom to negotiate a better placement. **The three tiers are:**

- Preferred risk
- Standard risk
- Substandard risk

Ideally, you want to fall into the top tier. The insurance provider looks at four criteria to establish your category of risk:

- **Your present health status:** Through a medical history and the needed medical exam, the insurance provider classifies you into one of the groups. A personal history of sickness places you in a high-risk group. If your health has been excellent, you qualify at a higher level, which translates into reduced rates.

  The insurance company also asks about your family's medical history, including the ages at which your parents, grandparents, and/or siblings died. If your parents died at very early ages or if one or both of them had significant conditions such as cancer, heart disease, or diabetes, you may fall into a higher risk group.

- **Your predicted health status:** Your present health status, your personal medical history, and your family's medical history (see the previous item) all show how much danger you have of dying sooner than the statistics estimate based on your current age. Because the insurance company is wagering that you'll live longer than projected, a positive prediction indicates that you'll either pay your premiums for a longer time or you'll cancel your insurance at some point. Either way, the firm gets used to the money and never has to pay it off.

- **Your job:** Some vocations are just riskier than others. The degree to which your work throws you into a high-risk group (not too many do, by the way), translates into the amount of your premium. Changing professions or vocations isn't an option for most individuals, and doing so merely to save money on a life insurance premium is foolish. Nevertheless, you should recognize that your employer does have an influence.

- **Exceptional conditions:** If the insurance company detects any odd or special situations, it will investigate. If, for example, you suddenly for no apparent reason acquire a $5 million policy while you're in your 20s, the insurance company may ask a few more questions than normal. Likewise, if you make a declaration in your application that disagrees with other assertions. If the corporation isn't pleased with your responses, the underwriter will ask you to elaborate. And in certain situations, the insurance company may even engage detectives who would ask inquiries of family members, neighbors, and acquaintances. The degree to which you can address any unexpected conditions without having to demand an inquiry makes you more insurable at a reduced premium cost.

Comparing Rates and Companies

Chapter 8 addresses how to pick the firm from whom you purchase your life insurance policy. This section provides methods you can utilize to assist you to reach the bottom line.

Comparing the costs of term insurance to cash-value plans is nearly difficult.

When you're ready to start looking for life insurance, do the following:

- **Pick which sort of insurance:** The first thing you must do is decide which kind of coverage you want (if you could afford it): term, whole life, universal life, or variable life. You must also pick which riders if any, you want. Review the material in the preceding chapters, which describe the intricacies of each sort of policy and rider, and go through the pluses and minuses of each.

- **Look for insurance firms**: Seek out at least five or six businesses and/or brokers who offer the sort of coverage you desire. Use the information in Chapter 8 to help you rate the insurance firms. Eliminate any businesses that you have reservations about. If you chat with any independent agents, remember to find out whose business would be underwriting your insurance.

- **Ask for quotations from each of those remaining businesses or agents:** Be assured that each quote reflects the same amount of death benefit with all the same riders/options you desire. If feasible, ask the agent or firm to break out the costs so you may more readily compare the plans which is especially critical when you analyze cash-value insurance.

If you're undecided as to which form of insurance to purchase, acquire quotations for all kinds of plans. Only then can you correctly judge which one is ideal for you.

Keys to comparing term insurance plans

- The rate for the first year does not necessarily represent the overall cost of the insurance: Many firms lower the first premiums to win your business, but the total cost over a long time is greater than from other companies. If you want to be insured for 20 or 30 years, make sure to add the estimated rates for the following three or four periods (terms, not years).

- If the firm provides dividends, check out the history of the distributions so that you can properly depend on the estimates.

- **Compare the same categories of risk:** If one firm quotes you a preferred rate while another company quotes you the standard rate, you're not necessarily comparing the prices. On the other hand, if the firms will genuinely vary in the area of risk, utilizing the quotation they will give is vital.

- Compare the term insurance prices with the cash-value insurance costs: If you believe you may wish to purchase a cash-value policy in the future, you may obtain a lower rate while converting with the same insurance provider than purchasing a new policy.

Keys to comparing entire life insurance plans

- **Premiums stay constant for the whole policy:** To compare expenses and prices, you must compare the mortality charges, cash values, dividends, and death benefits.

- Although one firm may pay a dividend and another may not, the dividend-paying company is not always the superior buy: You can determine only after you have bid.

- Take the predicted cash-value profits with a grain of salt: Companies typically offer you charts boasting high expected returns. Use the guaranteed return for your comparisons.

Because profits on whole life insurance are tax-deferred, you must consider your after-tax return, not simply the return itself when comparing the return on your policy to a return on a taxable investment. To calculate the after-tax return, you have to know your marginal tax rate (including your state income tax if applicable) (including your state income tax if applicable).

If you're in the 28 percent federal income tax bracket and the 7 percent state income tax bracket, it implies that 28 + 7, or 35 percent of a taxable return on investment will be paid to the government. By removing the total tax paid from the total return, you obtain your after-tax return. So a 10 percent taxable return is the same as a 6.5 percent untaxed return (35 percent of 10 is 3.5, which, when deducted from 10, leaves 6.5). (35 percent of 10 is 3.5, which, when subtracted from 10, leaves 6.5).

- Put more stock into the insurance company's rating: With term insurance, you're simply worried that the firm stays solvent for the time you purchase, but with your whole life, you're investing into the company itself. A firm with a much lower rating may promise a somewhat better return, but you may want to carefully examine the lesser-yielding but the higher-rated company for your peace of mind.

- Insurance is protection, not investment: If you want to get a whole life insurance because you believe it's a smart investment, think again. Many alternative assets such as IRAs and 401(k)s may provide you a greater and still tax-deferred return on your dollar. You may be just as well off putting your money in another tax-deferred vehicle and getting a lower-cost term insurance policy.

- Find out what happens if you discontinue your coverage: Some insurance firms have cancellation or termination costs, while others put in administrative expenses upfront. Include these costs in your comparisons.

Keys to comparing universal life insurance products

Universal life insurance is comparable to whole life; nevertheless, several factors make universal life policies more difficult to compare with each other. To compare policies and riders by using the Universal Life Worksheet in Chapter 6, remember these four keys (Note: You may use these same keys when comparing variable life insurance plans):

- Premiums for universal life don't always stay constant for the whole policy (unlike whole life): Therefore, to compare costs and rates, you have to utilize the same premium.

- The death benefit in universal life insurance may either stay constant or rise as your cash value increases: Use the same death benefit choice with each policy to compare costs and rates with different businesses and policies.

- Insurance firms will present you with both assured and optimistic expected earnings: Take these hopeful predictions with a grain of salt. Use the promised profits, and if you receive more, consider it a bonus. On the other side, you can also examine the company's history payback to get a notion of whether the rosy estimates are pie-in-the-sky or rather realistic.

- Put the additional stock into the insurance company's rating: With universal and whole life, you're purchasing into the firm itself. If one firm promises a little more but has a much lower rating, you may want to carefully consider the lower-yielding but better-rated organization.

- Insurance is protection, not investment: Many alternative assets may provide you a greater return on your dollar than universal life insurance, including IRAs and 401(k)s, both of which offer the same tax-deferred advantage. You may be just as well off placing money in other tax-deferred assets and getting a lower-cost term insurance policy.

CHAPTER EIGHT

LIFE INSURANCE PROVISIONS AND OPTIONS

IN THE I S CHAPTER

- Determining your death benefit payout possibilities
- Reading the tiny print for provisions and exclusions
- Terminating your policy
- Filing a claim

This chapter addresses some of the important articles in a typical life insurance policy and emphasizes some of the crucial characteristics that you should look for. This chapter also outlines the settlement choices that are available to your beneficiaries, gives example benefit tables for life income benefits, and describes how to make a claim.

Follow this simple rule: Don't sign anything that you don't comprehend!

Ownership

Your insurance policy is property, and you own it. The policy is real and has value, even if you have a term life insurance policy. That implies that you have certain rights linked with ownership. Among them are

- **The right to pick your beneficiaries:** As the owner of the insurance policy, you get to determine who is the beneficiary after you die. You may alter the beneficiary, given that you face no other legal constraints, such as divorce settlements in which your dependent children are expressly specified as beneficiaries.

- **The right to cancel your insurance:** If you wish, you may terminate your policy at any stage, either by written notification or by failing to make premium payments. You should remember, however, that with certain cash-value plans, any surrender value goes toward paying the premium. In addition, you may be asked to pay cancellation costs.

- **The right to convert your policy, if you purchase that right as a rider:** If you acquire a term life insurance policy but include a rider that lets you change to a cash-value policy at a later date without any further requirements, you may choose for this conversion at your discretion. Note: If you raise the death benefit or face value, the firm may force you to take a new medical exam and re-qualify, which contradicts the entire point of obtaining the conversion rider.

- **The right to cash in your surrender value at any time:** Just as you have the right to cancel your policy, you have the right to take out any cash value you accumulate, less any cancellation costs or administrative expenses.

- The right to exercise any choices that your policy includes: If you include any riders or options in your policy, you may dictate how and when these options are exercised. With death benefit payments, however, your best chance may be to leave as many choices open for your survivors as possible so that they may utilize the death benefit to meet their requirements.

Death Benefit Payment Options

Most people think that when a person who has life insurance dies, the beneficiaries immediately receive a cheque in the mail as payment on the insured person's death benefit.

Nothing can be farther from the truth. The insurance business must be told when one of its policyholders has died; normally, such communication must be in the form of a certified copy of a formal death certificate with an embossed seal. See "Filing a Claim," later in this chapter, for more information.

Although executors of estates usually take care of these matters, that's not always the case. So if your loved one dies and you know that he or she has a current insurance policy, be careful to follow up so that the beneficiary may get the payout. If you need to receive official copies of the death certificate, you may typically get copies for a modest price from the funeral home or whoever performed the burial or cremation.

Taking a lump-sum payment

The lump-sum payout is the most usual, although death benefits are provided to recipients in other ways, too.

Choosing installment payments

As the life insurance policyholder, you may choose that your beneficiary is to be paid the death benefit a bit at a time, over several years.

You may pick whether you wish to set a certain period for these payments or that a specified amount be paid in each payment until the entire death benefit runs out. Any money that hasn't yet been paid creates interest.

In most instances, this income is not taxable to the beneficiary, although you and your beneficiary should certainly check with a tax advisor before making that assumption.

Maintaining the principle:
Interest-only payments

You can specify that your beneficiary gets a periodic payment of the interest on the death benefit's cash value. Because the beneficiary earns interest on the account, he or she must claim the benefit as taxable income. An interest-only payment option is a means of budgeting the funds while maintaining the investment. Beneficiaries typically have the option of withdrawing the principal (although normally not all at once), which contradicts the objective of this payment option. Or they may borrow against the principle by using it as collateral and earn a higher rate than they can get from a bank loan. Usually, the life insurance policy sets a minimum interest rate.

Making it last: Payments for life
Another payment option is a payment-for-life scheme. As with the interest-only option, your recipient receives a monthly payment from the death benefit, which is a manner of budgeting the money while keeping an investment. However, the amount the beneficiary gets is depending on the conditions you put up, the total amount of the death benefit and cash

value, and the length of time you designate for the payments. With this option, the beneficiary can't withdraw the funds but is guaranteed payment for a specified period of his or her lifetime.

Note that the amount is depending on the beneficiary's age and sex and whether you designate several years of payment or if you leave the number of years open.

As long as the recipient is alive, he or she gets equal amounts after each monthly interval. If you specify a certain period, then payments continue as long as the recipient lives or until the end of the set term, whichever is longer. If the beneficiary dies within the set term, that person's heirs receive a lump sum payment of any debt outstanding

Joining together: Joint life income

This plan employs a schedule of payments that mixes the two beneficiaries' ages and sexes. The beneficiary gets payments as long as one of the two payees is alive.

Setting up special options

If you wish to set up any other form of the payment plan, that's up to you and the insurance provider. As long as whatever arrangements you want to make are legal, companies are usually willing to set them up. However, more than likely, they will charge a little extra for this inventive arrangement since they may have to perform some legal work.

In general, insurance providers don't advocate that you build up your payment alternatives unless you have an attorney examine them. The insurance and tax regulations involve numerous complexities (and, of course, they're continually being amended); you may easily select a creative payment scheme without understanding that you've created more barriers for your beneficiaries than you want to. Many lawyers are fairly aware of different methods to choose how your heirs get your death benefits.

Provisions and Exclusions

Every insurance policy is normally in tiny type several paragraphs that are vital for you to read. Basically, in addition to some rather obvious notions (such as, "all amounts paid will be in United States dollars"), these lines describe all the reasons you would not be protected that is, reasons your beneficiaries would not receive any of the cash you explicitly designated for them.

Age and sex

This clause is a mechanism for the insurance company to protect itself if it (or you) made a mistake, identifying you either as the incorrect sex or as older as or younger than you were at the time of application. The insurance company lists these two characteristics since they're the two important aspects of how much it costs you for protection. The insurance company adjusts the policy benefits for the correct age or sex.

Suicide

Just nearly every life insurance application has a suicide clause. This clause doesn't exclude all benefits if you commit suicide. Rather, it specifies that if you die as a result of suicide within two years from the issue date of the policy, your beneficiaries are not eligible for the death benefit (which may be referred to as the Amount of Basic Plan) (which may be referred to as the Amount of Basic Plan).

In addition, most policies also specify that if you do commit suicide within two years, your beneficiaries will receive an amount equal to the premiums you paid on the policy from the starting date, called the date of issuance, to the date of death by suicide.

War

Although some policies specifically exclude paying death benefits when you die from injuries sustained during a war whether you belong to the military or not many policies do not. On the other side, plans generally exclude the waiver of premium benefits if you become fully handicapped as a consequence of war.

Non-commercial aviation

Many plans would exclude a death benefit if you die as a consequence of a noncommercial aircraft accident, meaning an airplane flight for which no fees are needed.

Dangerous activities

If you die while engaging in an inherently dangerous activity, such as skydiving or hang gliding, your policy may not cover you. Check the small print to make certain some plans don't exclude the activity but do charge higher rates if you disclose that you partake in these sorts of activities.

Incontestability clause

A major component in most life insurance plans is the incontestability clause. This condition stipulates that save for non-payment of premiums, the firm will not question either the policy or the waiver of premium clause once the policy has been in effect for a specific time, generally two years. So if the company discovers an error in your application after that period, it can't go back and void your policy. This provision protects you even if you misrepresent yourself on your application, unless you falsify your age or gender, as mentioned previously in this chapter.

Premium provisions

The policy must specify how the premiums are payable and when they are due. The policy also must specify whether you have a grace period and, if so, how long the period lasts. During the grace period, the insurance company usually extends your coverage. If you don't pay your premium by the end of the grace period, the insurance company will first turn to whatever dividends it owes you to repay the cost of the premium. If you don't have any dividend or if the dividend is inadequate, the policy expires and your coverage terminates. You remain covered until the insurance is officially terminated.

Next, the policy states whether any cash value will be used to pay the premium and, if so, how you will be notified.

Finally, the policy states how long you have to apply for reinstatement if your policy lapses. This time may be as long as five years after the policy terminates, however you will generally have to present evidence that you're still insurable.

Furthermore, you will have to pay all the unpaid premiums plus com- hammered interest, as indicated in the insurance contract (about 6 percent each year).

Termination

As the word termination suggests, the policy stipulates when the death benefit, all riders, and the waiver of premium benefit will terminate.

Filing a Claim

When a loved one dies, thinking about the life insurance policy may seem callous. Yet, oddly, thinking about life insurance might bring a huge amount of comfort. A loved one's death brings many things to think about and numerous costs that are unanticipated and, frequently, prohibitive. The cost of the funeral itself averages $5,000 to $10,000 and can be much more, and along with that expense (and others) comes the immediate loss of income.

The good news here is that filing a life insurance claim is very easy, even if you don't have all the details about the policy. It's easy even if you don't have the actual policy!

Steps to filing a claim

Here's how to submit a life insurance policy claim:

1. Look around to see whether you can find the written policy.

2. Call the insurance agent who sold your loved one the coverage. If no agent is named or you don't know who the agent is, contact the firm itself (or any local representative

for the company, who will either connect you to the right claims agent or handle it herself) (or any local agent for the company, who will either get you to the appropriate claims agent or handle it herself).

3. Fill out the paperwork and forms as required. The insurance agent can normally complete much of this chore for you, but the forms should be very straightforward, particularly if you have the policy itself handy.

4 Get a certified copy of the death certificate.

5. Submit the claim form with the death certificate. In only a matter of a few days to a week or two, you get your compensation.

Choosing among settlement options

The most challenging element of the claim procedure is choosing the settlement option you want if the policyholder hasn't already picked the payment plan. You may generally pick from multiple possibilities.

Take great attention to these two things:

- You may arrange to have the funeral costs paid immediately from the proceeds of your insurance policy. The funeral director will arrange for this payment.

- If you know your loved one was covered but you don't have the policy or know the name of the insurance company that provided the policy, you may be able to receive the essential information by calling the American Council of

Life Insurance at 1001 Pennsylvania Ave. NW, Washington, DC 20004. The Council will transmit your query to roughly 100 of the top insurance firms in the nation so that they may explore if your loved one had a policy with them.

Personal Home Insurance

Insurance for your home offers financial security against mishaps. Since it is a flat-rate policy, bodily injury and property damage caused by the insured or his families to third parties are both covered. It also covers civil liability. This includes harm brought on by animals.

There are some exceptions, but most accidents result in damage that is covered. Floods, earthquakes, and negligent maintenance are not typically covered by homeowner's insurance. However, the National Flood Insurance Program (NFIP) and some private insurers offer flood coverage as a separate policy. You can purchase earthquake insurance as a separate policy or as an endorsement. For the majority of maintenance issues, owners are accountable.

Four fundamental types of coverage are typically included in a home insurance policy. They include:

1. **Shielding the home's framework**
   If your home is damaged or destroyed by a fire, hurricane, hail, lightning, or any other disaster listed in the policy, this section of the insurance covers the costs of repairing or rebuilding it. Flooding, earthquakes, or regular wear and tear are not covered. The majority of common policies also include detached buildings like a garage, tool shed, or

garden shed. Usually, 10% of the cost of house insurance goes toward covering these constructions.

2. **Personal property coverage**

   If your personal belongings are stolen or damaged in a fire, storm, or other insured catastrophe, you are still protected. This includes furniture, clothes, sporting goods, and other stuff. The majority of businesses provide 50 to 70 percent of the cost of homeowner's insurance. Off-site protection is covered by this clause of the insurance. If the insured choose not to have coverage outside of the premises, the property is protected anywhere in the globe. Silverware, furs, and other pricey objects are insured, although there are often monetary restrictions in the event of theft. People may either acquire a separate list of personal property or float and insure the item at its assessed value in order to fully insure these goods.

   Standard house insurance also provides coverage for trees, plants, and shrubs, often up to $500 per item. Theft, fire, lightning, explosion, vandalism, rioting, and even aircraft disasters are among the dangers addressed. They are not protected from illness or wind damage.

3. **Protection from liability**

   Liability insurance covers the expenses of claims for physical harm or property damage caused to third parties by the insured or members of their family. Pet-related damage is also covered. Up to the policy limit, the liability insurance portion of the policy covers any court judgments and the expenses of the insured's legal defense. There is worldwide coverage in addition to domestic coverage. Liability limits often begin at $100,000. However, experts advise homeowners to get at least $300,000 worth of coverage. The insurance may be expanded by adding an umbrella or deductible policy, which offers larger liability limits and wider coverage that includes slander and defamation claims. Roof plans typically cost between $200 and $350 for an extra $1 million in liability insurance.

Health insurance without debt is often included in home insurance packages. The injured individual only has to submit their medical costs to the insured's insurance provider if they are hurt at home.

In this manner, the expenses are covered without any legal action being taken. The insured's family or pets' medical bills, however, are not covered by this insurance.

4. **Additional costs of living**
   If the house is inhabitable as a result of damage from a fire, storm, or other insured disaster, this pays for the increased expenses of living away from home. It pays for hotel costs, dining out, and any extra living costs incurred while the home restoration. The amount of extra living costs that are covered varies from business to business. About 20% of house insurance is covered by many plans. For an extra fee, coverage may be expanded. For a brief period of time, some businesses provide policies with limitless loss of use coverage.

Additionally, homeowners who rent out a part of their property are compensated for the rent that the renter would have paid in the event that the residence had not been damaged through Supplemental Living Expense Coverage.

Types of Home Insurance

There are numerous forms of house insurance that varies in the amount of insurance coverage they give. The diverse types are quite typical across the nation. However, nations and individual firms may provide typefaces that are somewhat different or have distinct names, such as "standard" or "deluxe". People who rent the residences they live in have particular renting restrictions.

Here are numerous forms of house insurance.

- HO-3: This is the most prevalent regulation that protects the house against all threats except those expressly prohibited.

- HO-1: restricted coverage policy
  This basic coverage offers protection for the first 10 claims. No longer available in most countries.

- HO-2: fundamental policy
  The standard policy offers protection against all 16 accidents. There is a variant of the HO-2 built for mobile homes.

- HO-8: Old house
  Designed for older properties, this coverage generally compensates damages based on real cash worth, which is replacement prices minus depreciation. A complete replacement cost coverage may not be provided for certain older properties.

- HO4: Tenant
  Created primarily for those who rent the place they reside in, this insurance covers personal possessions and any component of the flat that the insured owns, such as freshly fitted kitchen cabinetry, against 16 claims.

- H0-6: Apartment/Cooperative
  A condominium or co-ownership insurance covers the property and construction elements of the building that they own. Protects against 16 calamities.

What types of claims are covered?

Most home insurance policies cover the 16 catastrophes listed below. Some basic rules cover only the first 10:

- ❖ Fire or lightning
- ❖ Storm or hail
- ❖ Explosion
- ❖ Riots or civil disturbances
- ❖ Damage caused by the aircraft
- ❖ Damage caused by vehicles
- ❖ Smoking
- ❖ Vandalism or malicious intent
- ❖ Flight
- ❖ Volcanic eruption
- ❖ Drop-down item
- ❖ Weight of ice, snow or sleet
- ❖ Accidental spillage or overflow of water or steam from plumbing, heating, air conditioning or fire protection systems, or from appliances

- Sudden and accidental cracking, bursting, burning or bulging of a steam or hot water heating system, air conditioning system or automatic fire protection system
- Freezing of plumbing, heating, air conditioning or automatic systems, sprinkler systems or appliances
- Sudden and accidental damage due to artificially generated electric current (excluding loss of tubes, transistors or similar electronic components)

Default owner rule exclusions

A standard homeowner's policy excludes coverage for floods, earthquakes, war, nuclear accidents, landslides, landslides and sinkholes. Here are some exclusions described below.

1. **Floods**

   Flood damage is excluded from standard homeowner's and renter's insurance policies. However, flood coverage is available as a separate policy from the National Flood Insurance Program (NFIP) and some private insurers. Additional information about flood insurance can be found at FloodSmart.gov or by calling 888-379-9531. For coverage above the $250,000 property and $100,000 contents limits provided by the NFIP, private insurance companies offer flood insurance. Tsunamis cause flood damage and are therefore only covered by a flood insurance policy.

2. **Earthquakes**

   Earthquake coverage can be a separate policy or add-on to a homeowner's or renter's policy. It is available from most insurance companies. In California, it is also available through the California Earthquake Authority, a privately funded government organization. In earthquake-prone states like California, the policy carries a high deductible.

3. Damages resulting from "faulty, defective or improper" care, workmanship, construction or materials
   Defective products may contain construction materials. The insurance policy does not cover damage due to lack of maintenance, mold, termite infestation and other pests. The policyholder is obliged to take reasonable precautions to protect the property from damage.

Coverage levels

There are three coverage options.

1. **Actual cash value**
   This type of coverage pays to replace the home or property minus the depreciation deduction.

2. **Replacement cost:**
   This type of coverage pays for the cost of rebuilding or repairing the home or replacing the property without deducting the capital expense allowance.

3. **Guaranteed/extended replacement cost**
   A full replacement cost policy pays a certain percentage, usually 20-25%, above the coverage limit to rebuild the home in the event of an increase in material and labor costs due to, for example, a widespread disaster. For example, if owners purchase a $100,000 policy, they can get up to $20,000 or $25,000 in additional coverage.

Some companies offer a guaranteed replacement cost policy, which will pay for whatever is needed to restore the home to what it was before the fire or other disaster, even if it exceeds the policy limit. This protects against sudden increases in construction costs due to shortages of building materials after a major disaster or other unforeseen circumstances. It generally does not cover the cost of upgrading the house in accordance with the applicable building regulations. However, an endorsement (or amendment) of the policy, called an ordinance or law, can help pay for these additional costs.

Extended and guaranteed replacement costs are more expensive; but it can provide excellent financial protection against disasters. However, this type of coverage may not be available in all states or with all carriers.

CHAPTER NINE

BASICS OF COMMERCIAL INSURANCE

Most companies must have at least the following four types of insurance:

1. **Content assurance**

   Home insurance reimburses businesses if property used in the business is lost or damaged due to various types of common perils, such as fire or theft. Property insurance covers not only the building or structure, but also its contents, including office furniture, inventory, raw materials, machinery, computers and other items essential to business operations. Depending on the type of policy, property insurance can cover equipment breakdown, debris removal after a fire or other devastating event, certain types of water damage, and other losses.

Business interruption insurance

Business interruption insurance, also known as business income insurance, is a type of property insurance. A business whose property has suffered direct physical damage, such as a fire or a roof damaged by a tree that fell in a storm, and must close completely while the facilities are repaired, could lose it to the competition. Rapid recovery of business activities after a disaster is crucial. This is why business loss insurance is so important.

There are generally three types of professional indemnity insurance. A company can buy one or a combination of these.

- **Business Income Cover:** Covers loss of income if the business has to vacate its premises due to damage related to a loss covered by a home insurance policy. Business income insurance covers the profit that the company would have made, based on financial data, if the disaster had not occurred. The policy also covers operational costs, such as electricity, that continue even if business is temporarily interrupted.

- **Additional revenue coverage:** reimburses the business a reasonable amount it spends, in addition to normal operating costs, to avoid closure during the recovery period.

- **Business Interruption Insurance:** Protects the business owner's profits after physical loss or damage to the assets of the insured's suppliers or customers, as opposed to their own assets.

Damage caused by floods, earthquakes and acts of terrorism are generally not covered by standard commercial property insurance, but can be purchased in a variety of markets.

Protection against flood damage

Home insurance generally excludes flood damage coverage. Businesses should check with their local government office or commercial bank whether their business is located in a flood-prone area and whether their location has flooded in the past. Flood insurance is available through the federal government's National Flood Insurance Program, which is operated by private companies and some specialty insurers.

Earthquake protection

Coverage for damage caused by earthquakes is excluded from most property insurance policies, including business owner's insurance policies. Businesses located in an earthquake-prone area need special earthquake insurance or an earthquake approval for business premises.

Protection against losses due to terrorist attacks

Under the Terrorism Risk Insurance Act 2002 and its extensions, only companies that take out optional terrorism cover are covered against losses caused by acts of terrorism. The exception is workers' compensation, which covers work-related injuries and deaths, including those caused by acts of terrorism.

2. **Liability insurance**

   Any company can be sued. Customers can claim that a company has harmed them because of, for example, a defective product, service failure, or neglect of the property of others. Or the complainant may allege that the company created an unsafe environment. Liability insurance covers damages for which the company is liable, up to policy limits, as well as attorneys' fees and other legal defense costs. It also pays medical bills for anyone injured by or on company property.

Commercial General Liability (CGL) insurance is the first line of defense against common claims. **CGL policies cover claims in four basic categories of commercial liability:**

- Physical injury
- Material damage
- Personal injury (including libel or slander)
- Advertising damage (damage due to defamation or false advertising)

In addition to covering the claims listed above, CGL policies also cover the costs of defending or settling claims. Liability insurance always indicates the maximum amount that the insurer will pay during the duration of the insurance. There are two main types of liability insurance that a company can choose: accidental damage and reported damage. Both of the policies have their advantages.

- **Accident Policy** – The insurance policy covers the business for damage caused to third parties by incidents that occur while the policy is in force, regardless of when the claim is made. For example, a person might sue a company in 2010 for an injury resulting from a fall in 1999. The policies in place at the time of the incident (i.e., 1999) will apply even if the company now has a policy with higher limits. Accident cover may not be available in certain states or for certain industries or occupations.

- **Indemnity Policy:** A loss insurance policy covers the company in accordance with the policy in force at the time of the claim, regardless of when the incident occurred. In the example above, the current policy limits apply to 2010. Companies with an indemnity policy can purchase optional "terminal coverage." Additional coverage allows the company to file claims after the policy expires for alleged injuries that occurred while the policy was in force.

3. **Company car insurance**

   A commercial auto insurance policy covers vehicles that are primarily used in commercial facilities or business activities. The insurance compensates all costs to third parties resulting from bodily injuries or material damage for which the company is legally responsible within the limits of the policy.

   Although the main coverage's are the same, commercial auto policies differ from passenger auto policies in several technical ways. They may have greater restrictions and/or provisions for leased vehicles and other non-owned vehicles, including employee cars used for company business. Several insurers offer commercial auto policies aimed at small business owners or certain types of businesses.

4. **Employee compensation insurance**

   Employers have a legal responsibility to their employees to make the workplace safe. Despite precautions, accidents can still happen. To protect employers from lawsuits arising from workplace accidents and to provide medical care and compensation for lost wages to employees injured in workplace accidents, companies in almost all states are required by law to purchase workers' compensation insurance. Workplace compensation insurance covers employees injured on the job, whether they are injured on a construction site or elsewhere, or as a result of road traffic accidents at work. It also includes occupational diseases. Workers' compensation provides payments to injured workers regardless of who caused the accident, lost time at work, and medical and rehabilitation services. It also provides death benefits to surviving spouses and survivors.

Each state has different laws governing the amount and duration of earnings loss benefits, the provision of medical and rehabilitation services, and how the system is administered. For example, most states have regulations about whether an employee or employer can choose which doctor will treat injuries and how compensation disputes are resolved.

Workers' compensation insurance must be purchased as a separate policy. Home and business owner policies (BOP) are sold as comprehensive policies, but do not include employee injury coverage.

Other types of commercial hedges

The first four coverage described below are different types of liability insurance available to businesses. The fifth form is life insurance. There are also specialized liability policies aimed at certain types of businesses.

1. **Errors and omissions/Professional liability insurance**
   Some businesses include services such as giving advice, making recommendations, designing things, providing physical care, or representing the needs of others, which can result in clients or patients suing them alleging that the

company's inability to properly perform the task caused them harm. Errors and omissions or professional indemnity insurance covers these situations. The policy compensates all judgments for which the insured is legally responsible, up to the policy limit. It also covers legal defense costs, even in the absence of fault.

2. **Liability insurance for work practices**
   Employment liability insurance covers, up to policy limits, damages for which the employer is legally liable, such as a violation of an employee's civil or legal rights. In addition to paying the judgment for which the insured is responsible, it also covers legal defense costs, which can be significant even if no fault has been committed.

3. **Civil liability insurance for directors and corporate officers**
   Directors' and officers' liability insurance protects directors and officers of businesses or non-profit organizations in the event of a lawsuit alleging that they managed the business or organization without regard for the rights of others. The policy compensates all judgments for which the insured is legally responsible, up to the policy limit. It also provides for legal defense costs, even if no wrongdoing has been committed.

4. **Roof policy or franchise**
   As the name suggests, a general liability insurance policy provides coverage in addition to the company's other liability coverage. It is designed to protect against abnormally high losses and provides protection when the limits of one of the underlying policies are exhausted. For a typical business, an

umbrella policy would provide protection beyond your general liability and personal liability policy. If the business has professional indemnity, directors' indemnity, or other types of liability insurance, an umbrella may also provide protection beyond the policy limits. The costs depend on the nature of the company, its size, the type of risks the company faces and the way the company implements risk reduction.

5. **Life insurance of a key person**

   Losing a key person can be a big blow to a small business if that person is the founder of the company or the primary point of contact for customers, suppliers and company management. The loss of a key person can also make the business less efficient and lead to a loss of capital. Losses caused by the death of a key employee can be insured. These policies indemnify the company for significant losses due to the death or disability of that person. The amount and cost of insurance required for a particular job depends on the situation and the age, health and role of the key employee. A key employee's life insurance policy pays a death benefit to the company after the key employee's death. The policy is usually owned by the company that pays the premiums and is the beneficiary. Key-person insurance money can be used to buy back company stock from the deceased's estate, pay a recruiting firm to find a suitable replacement, and cover costs or expenses while the company adjusts to the loss.

Package Policy

Commercial insurers sell coverage separately and/or offer policies that protect against most major property and liability risks in one package. Global policies are created for types of business that generally present the same type and degree of risk.

1. **Small business plans**

   Small businesses often purchase a comprehensive policy known as a Business Owner's Policy or BOP. BOP is recommended for most small businesses (typically 100 employees or less) because it is often the cheapest way to get comprehensive coverage. BOPs are **"off-the-shelf"** policies that combine many of the basic coverage a typical small business needs in a standard package at a premium that is usually lower than that required to purchase these coverage separately. Combining both property insurance and liability insurance, BOP covers business for property damage, business interruption, lawsuits resulting from bodily injury or damage to the property of others, etc. BOP does not cover professional liability, auto insurance, and workers 'compensation. That is, health and disability insurance. Small businesses need separate insurance policies to cover professional services, vehicles and employees.

2. **Multiple commercial policies**

   Large companies can purchase a commercial insurance policy or tailor their policies to the specific risks they face. Commercial comprehensive policies, often bought by businesses, include property, boiler and machinery, criminal and general liability cover. An employee of a large company is a risk manager who helps determine the company's exposure to certain risks.

3. **Parent company policy**
   There are several insurance options designed to meet the unique needs of home-based businesses.

- Owner's Driver Policy - Owners can add a single rider or driver to an existing owner's policy to increase coverage.

- Commercial Home Insurance Policy - A commercial home insurance policy provides more comprehensive coverage for equipment and business liability than a home insurance policy. Many insurance companies offer insurance policies specifically designed for small businesses.

- **Business Policy (BOP):** the parent company can benefit from the Business Policy (BOP), see above. The key to determining whether a business owner qualifies for a BOP is the size of the facility, the required liability limits, the type of business activity, and the extent of outsourcing and processing activities. BOP, like a home business policy, covers business property and equipment, loss of income, additional expenses and liability; however, BoP offers these coverages on a much broader scale.

CHAPTER TEN

BASIC PRINCIPLES OF LIFE INSURANCE

Many financial experts consider life insurance to be a cornerstone of good financial planning. It can be very helpful in the following situations:

1. **Replacement of income from the closest relatives**
   If people depend on a person's income, life insurance can replace that income if the person dies. The most famous example is that of parents with small children. Income replacement insurance can be particularly useful if your surviving spouse or partner's government or employer benefits are reduced after your death.

2. **Pay the final fees**
   Life insurance policies can pay for funeral and burial expenses, estate and other property administration expenses, debts and medical expenses not covered by health insurance.

3. **Create a legacy for heirs**
   Even those who have no other assets to pass on can create an inheritance by purchasing life insurance and naming their heirs as beneficiaries.

4. **Pay the federal "death" tax and the state "death" tax.**
   Life insurance benefits help pay inheritance tax so heirs don't have to liquidate other assets or receive a smaller inheritance. Changes to federal estate tax rules by January 1, 2011 will likely reduce the impact of this tax on some people, but some states are making up for these federal reductions by raising state taxes.

5. **Make significant charitable contributions**
   By designating a charity as the beneficiary of their life insurance policies, individuals can make a much larger contribution than if they had donated the cash equivalent of the policy premiums.

6. **Create a source of savings**
   Certain types of life insurance policies create a cash value that, if not paid out as a death benefit, can be borrowed or withdrawn at the owner's request. Since most people place a high priority on paying premiums for their life insurance policy, purchasing a cash value policy can create a sort of "forced" savings plan. Interest accrued is also tax-free (and tax-free if the money is paid out as a death claim).

Types of life insurance

There are two main types of life insurance policies: term and whole life.

1. **Term life insurance**
   Term life insurance is the simplest form of life insurance. It only pays out if death occurs during the term of the policy, which is usually 1 to 30 years. Most term policies do not

have provisions for other benefits. There are two basic types of term life insurance policies: term and term. Deferral means that the death benefit remains the same for the duration of the policy. Expiration of the term means that the death benefit, usually in one-year increments, is reduced during the term.

2. **Whole life/permanent life**

   Whole or permanent life insurance pays a death benefit each time the insured person dies. There are three main types of permanent or whole life insurance: traditional whole life insurance, universal life insurance, and variable universal life insurance, and within each type there are variations.

   With traditional whole life insurance, the death benefit and premium are designed to remain the same (level) for the life of the policy. The cost per $1,000 of benefits increases as the insured ages and obviously becomes very high when the insured reaches age 80 or older. The insurance company maintains the premium level by charging a premium that is higher than what is needed to pay claims in the first few years, invests that money and then uses it to increase the premium level to help with the cost of life insurance for the elderly.

   When these "overpayments" reach a certain amount, the law must make them available to the insured as a surrender value if he decides not to continue with the original plan. The current value is an alternative benefit, not an add-on, according to the policy. In the 1970s and 1980s, life insurance companies introduced two variants of the traditional life insurance product: universal life insurance and variable universal life insurance.

Some variants of permanent life insurance/permanent life insurance are described below.

- **Universal life insurance:** Universal life insurance, also known as adjustable life insurance, offers more flexibility than traditional life insurance. The savings account (called a money account) generally earns interest in the money market. Once the money is in the account, the insured also has the option of adjusting the premium payment, as long as there is enough money in the account to cover the expenses.

- **Variable Life** – Variable life insurance plans combine death protection with a savings account that can be invested in stocks, bonds and money market mutual funds. Although the value of the policy grows faster, it carries more risk. If the investments do not perform well, the cash value and death benefit may be reduced. However, some policies guarantee that the death benefit will not fall below the minimum.

- **Variable Universal Life Insurance** - This type of policy combines the features of universal and variable life policies, including the investment risks and returns typical of variable life policies and the ability to adjust premiums and death benefits that are characteristic of Strategies universal life insurance.

Annuity Basics

Annuities are financial products designed to improve retirement security. An annuity is an arrangement in which a person or organization makes a series of payments to another person. Generally, the term "annuity" refers to a contract between an individual and a life insurance company.

There are many categories of annuities. They can be categorized according to:

- Nature of the underlying investment: fixed or variable
- Main purpose: capitalization or payment (deferred or immediate)
- Nature of payment obligation: fixed term, fixed amount or lifetime
- Tax status: qualified or non-qualified

Premium payment system: single premium or flexible premium

An annuity can fall into more than one of these categories at the same time. For example, a person may purchase a non-qualified deferred variable annuity with a single premium.

In general, annuities have the following characteristics:

1. **Deferral of tax on investment income**
   Many investments are taxable from year to year, but investment income (capital gains and investment income) in annuities is not taxable until the investor withdraws the money. This tax deferral also applies to 401(k) and IRA plans; However, unlike these products, there is no limit to

the amount that can be invested in an annuity. Also, the minimum withdrawal requirements for annuities are much more liberal than for 401(k)IRAs.

2. **Protection from creditors**
   People who have a current annuity (that is, who receive money from an insurance company) have some creditor protection. Generally, creditors have access to ongoing payments since the money the annuity owner gave to the insurance company now belongs to the company. Certain state laws and court rulings also protect some or all of these annuity payments.

3. **Diversity of investment opportunities**
   Vast majority of annuity companies offer a variety of investment options. For example, individuals can invest in a fixed annuity that credits a specific interest rate, similar to a bank certificate of deposit (CD). If they buy a variable annuity, they can invest their money in stocks, bonds or mutual funds. In recent years, annuity companies have created various types of "floors" that limit the extent to which an investment falls relative to a rising benchmark.

4. **Tax-free transfers between investment options**
   Unlike mutual funds and other investments made with after-tax money, annuities have no tax implications if owners change the way they invest their money. This can be especially helpful if they use a strategy called "rebalancing," which is recommended by many financial advisors. In rebalancing, investors periodically change their investments back to ratios that represent the most appropriate combination of risk and return for the investor's situation.

5. **Income for living**

   An immediate life annuity turns an investment into a series of payments that last until the annuitant's death. In concept, payouts come from three "pockets": the initial investment, the return on investment, and money from a group of people in a group of investors who don't live as long as the actuarial tables predict. Pooling is unique to annuities and allows annuity companies to guarantee income for life.

6. **Benefits for heirs**

   It is a common fear that if a person starts an annuity right away and dies soon after, the insurance company will keep the entire investment in the annuity. To avoid this situation, individuals can purchase a "guaranteed period" with an immediate annuity. The guaranteed period requires the insurance company to continue making payments after the owner's death to one or more designated beneficiaries; Payments continue until the end of the stated guarantee period, usually 10 or 20 years (measured from the time the owner began receiving annuity payments). Furthermore, annuity payments transferred to beneficiaries do not pass through the estate and are not determined by the will of the annuity owner.

Types of annuities

The two major types of annuities are the fixed and variable. Fixed annuities guarantee minimum capital and interest. Generally, accrued interest and fixed annuity payments are based on the company's stated rates, which can only change once a year. Fixed annuities are considered "general account" assets. Variable annuity and distribution account values, on the other hand, are based on the performance of an individual investment portfolio, so their value can vary daily. Variable annuities are considered "separate account" assets.

There are different fixed annuities and variable annuities. One example, an equity-indexed annuity, is a hybrid of fixed and variable income features.

Annuities have a minimum interest rate, like other fixed annuities, but their value is also based on the performance of a particular stock market index, which is calculated as part of that index's total return. In December 2008, the Securities and Exchange Commission voted to reclassify indexed annuities (with some exceptions) as securities rather than insurance products. Annuities can also be classified by marketing channels, i.e. whether they are sold to groups or individuals.

Annuities can be deferred or immediate. Deferred annuities typically accumulate assets over a long period of time, with withdrawals usually as a lump sum or income distribution after retirement. Payout annuities allow customers to turn a lump sum payment into income that the policyholder starts receiving immediately.

Basics of long-term care insurance

Dependency insurance reimburses the cost of assistance services for people who cannot perform certain activities of daily living without assistance or need supervision due to cognitive disorders such as Alzheimer's disease.

Features of long-term care policies

The best policies pay for care in a nursing home, care center or at home. Benefits are usually expressed in daily amounts, with a lifetime maximum. Some policies pay half a day for home care than for nursing home care. Others pay the same amount or have "perks" that can be used as needed.

Payment initiation criteria

The policy should specify the conditions that must be met. They can be:

1. **Inability to perform two or three specific "activities of daily living" without assistance**
   This includes washing, dressing, eating, going to the toilet and "moving" or being able to move from place to place or between bed and chair.

2. **Cognitive impairment**
   Most policies cover stroke, Alzheimer's disease and Parkinson's disease, but other forms of mental disability may be excluded.

3. **Medical need or doctor's confirmation that long-term care is needed**
   Most policies have a "waiting period" or "elimination period". It is the period that begins when a person first needs long-term care and lasts as long as determined by the policy. The policy will not pay benefits during the waiting period. The policy only reimburses costs incurred after the grace period has expired, if the insured still needs treatment. In

general, the longer the wait, the lower the long-term care premium.

Long-term care benefit periods can range from two years to a lifetime. Premiums can be kept low by choosing coverage for three to four years, longer than the average nursing home stay, instead of lifetime. Most long-term care policies are paid on a fee (or expense) basis, up to the policy limit. In other words, if the policy pays $150 per day, but the insured only spends $130 per day with the home care provider, the policy will only pay $130.

Some policies go into a "pool" of unused funds that can be used to extend the period the policy will pay benefits. Other policies are paid on a fee basis. Using the same example above, an indemnity policy would pay $150 per day as long as the insured needs and receives long-term care, regardless of the actual out-of-pocket cost.

Inflation protection is an important feature, especially for people under 65 who are buying benefits they may not use for 20 or more years. A good inflation supplement combines benefits at 5 percent per year. Without inflation protection, even a 3% annual inflation rate over 24 years will reduce the purchasing power of a $150 daily fee to the equivalent of $75.

Six other key policy provisions

1. **Waiting period**
   Under some policies, if the insured has eligible long-term care expenses on any day within a seven-day period, they

are credited with seven days for the elimination period: that is, the time between injury and landing. home care is often provided: some days by professionals and other days by family members.

2. **Guaranteed renewal policy**
   They must be renewed by the insurance company, although premiums may increase if they are increased for the entire class of insured.

3. **Waiver of premium**
   This provision ensures that premiums are no longer due after the insured receives payment.

4. **Notification to a third party**
   This provision states that a family member, friend or professional advisor will be notified if the insured forgets to pay the premium.

5. **No loss of profit**
   After these payments, the lower insurance amount remains in effect if the insured terminates the coverage. This provision is required by some states.

6. **Return of benefits**
   This provision ensures that the maximum benefits are withdrawn if the insured receives benefits for a period of time, then recovers and goes a certain period (usually six months) without receiving benefits.

CHAPTER ELEVEN

BASICS OF DISABILITY INSURANCE

Disabling injuries affect millions of Americans each year. Disability insurance, which is a supplement to health insurance, can replace lost income if a person is unable to work due to a disability.

There are three basic ways of income compensation.

1. **Professional disability insurance paid by the employer**
   This is mandatory in most states. Most employers offer short-term sick leave. Many large employers also offer long-term disability benefits, usually with benefits of up to 60% of salary for five years until age 65, and in some cases for life.

2. **Social security disability benefits**
   It is paid to employees whose incapacity for work should last at least 12 months and which is so serious that they cannot hope for gainful employment.

3. **Individual disability insurance**
   Other limited income replacements are available to employees under certain circumstances from workers'

compensation (if the injury or illness is work-related), auto insurance (if the disability is caused by a motor vehicle accident), and the Department of Veterans Affairs. For most employees, even those with employer-paid insurance, an individual disability income policy is the best way to ensure adequate income in the event of disability. Employees who purchase private disability insurance can expect to replace 50-70% of their income. Disability benefits paid on individual disability policies are not taxable; benefits paid by the employer are subject to income tax.

Types of disability insurance

There are two types of disability policies: short-term disability and long-term disability. Short-term policies have a grace period of 0 to 14 days with a maximum indemnity period of two years. Long-term policies have a waiting period of several weeks to several months with a maximum benefit period of several years for life.

Disability policies have two distinct protection features: irrevocable and guaranteed renewable. Irrevocable means that the insurance company cannot cancel the contract, except in case of non-payment of premiums. This gives the insured the right to renew the policy every year without increasing the premium or reducing the benefit. Guaranteed renewal allows the policyholder to renew the policy with the same benefits and not have a policy canceled by the company. However, the insurer has the right to increase premiums as long as it does so for all other policyholders of the same qualification class.

There are several options and factors to consider when purchasing a disability insurance policy.

1. **Additional purchase options**
   The insurance company gives the policyholder the right to subsequently take out additional insurance.

2. **Coordinate strengths**
   The amount of benefits insured persons receive from their insurance company depends on other benefits they receive as a result of the disability. Policy

   It determines the target amount that the insured will receive from all policies together and compensates for the unpaid difference from other policies.

3. **Cost of Living Adjustment (COLA)**
   COLA increases disability benefits over time based on increases in the cost of living as measured by the Consumer Price Index. Insureds pay a higher premium if they opt for COLA.

4. **Additional clause in case of residual or partial incapacity for work**
   This provision allows employees to return to part-time work, receive a portion of their wages, and receive partial disability benefits if they are still partially disabled.

5. **Refund of premium**
   This provision obliges the insurance company to refund part of the premium if no claim is filed within the time period specified in the policy.

6. **Determination of premium waiver**
   This clause means that the insured does not have to pay contractual premiums after 90 days of incapacity for work.

Factors influencing the choice of a disability insurance policy

1. **Definition of disability**
   Some policies pay benefits if employees are unable to perform the normal duties of their occupation. Others only pay if employees are unable to perform a job that matches their level of education and experience. Some policies define disability in terms of workers who are employed for an initial period of two or three years and then continue to pay benefits only if they are unable to work. Policies for independent housing are more desirable, but more expensive.

2. **Payment period**
   The benefit period is the time that policyholders receive on a monthly basis during their lifetime. Experts generally recommend that the policy pay benefits until at least age 65, after which Social Security takes over for disability. Younger people may want to consider buying a policy that offers lifetime benefits, as it will still be relatively inexpensive.

3. **Replacement rate:**
   A policy that replaces 60 to 70 percent of total taxable income is recommended. A higher replacement rate, if available, costs more. Other sources of income should be evaluated before making a decision on the required amount of disability insurance.

4. Insurance in case of incapacity to work due to accident or illness Accident insurance alone is cheaper, but does not provide sufficient protection. It would be ideal to take out accident insurance and health insurance.

5. **Increasing cost of living**
   The policy must not pay benefits for ten years or more and must keep pace with the rising cost of living. (Some companies also offer "indexed" benefits, which keep pace with inflation after benefits begin.)

6. **A policy that pays "remaining" or partial benefits**
   This type of policy is available so that people can work part-time and still receive benefits to compensate for lost income. Standard on some policies, and added by endorsement to others, a residual benefits policy pays partial benefits based on lost earnings without an initial period of total disability.

7. **Transitional benefits**
   It is offered by some companies, and can compensate for financial losses during the post-disability period in rebuilding a business or professional practice.

8. **Continuous coverage**
   An irrevocable policy remains in effect as long as the premium is paid; neither the benefit nor the premium can be changed. A guaranteed renewable policy retains the same benefits, but may cost more over time, as the insurer can increase the premium as it increases for the entire class of insured.

9. **Financial stability**

   Check the financial stability of the insurer through an agent or credit rating agency. Captives and other risk financing opportunities. Traditionally, businesses and other organizations have managed risk by transferring it to an insurance company through the purchase of an insurance policy or, alternatively, by retaining the risk and allocating funds to cover expected losses through a scheme called "self-insurance", in which businesses retain rather than transfer risk.

   During the liability crisis of the 1980s, when companies struggled to obtain certain types of commercial insurance, new risk transfer mechanisms were developed, facilitated by the passage of the Product Liability Retention Act of 1981. These so-called alternative risk transfer agreements (ARTs) combine mechanisms risk transfer and retention and together with self-insurance form an alternative market.

Alternative market mechanisms

I. **Prisoners**

   Privately held companies are companies created by large corporations to finance or manage their risk financing needs. If such a captive insures only the risks of its parent company or its subsidiaries, it is said to be a "pure" captive.

   Prisoners can be created to secure more than one entity. An association or group of companies can join together to form a closed insurance company. Professionals (doctors, lawyers, accountants) have trained many prisoners over the years. In turn, they can use various reinsurance mechanisms to provide coverage. In particular, many offshore inmates use a "border" insurance company to provide basic insurance. Fronting generally means that the underwriting, claims and administration work in the United States is handled by an experienced commercial insurance company, since the inmate generally does not want to be directly involved in the underwriting operation. In addition, the facade allows the business to demonstrate that it has an insurance policy with a licensed insurance company in the United States, which may be required for legal and business reasons.

The concept of self-financing income was introduced in Bermuda 20 years ago and remains a popular alternative market mechanism. Rent-a-captives focuses on companies that cannot capitalize on a captive, but are willing to bear a portion of their franchise and share insurance profits and investment income. The mechanism is usually sponsored by insurers or reinsurers, who essentially "rent out" their capital for a fee, and allows users to gain some of the benefits of a captive without paying the costs of setting up a captive. single parent inmate and with minimum equity and surplus requirements.

Captives have expanded into employee benefits since 2003, when the Labor Department gave final approval to Archer Daniels Midland Co.'s plan.

While the primary domicile of US captives is Vermont, offshore captives covering US risk are primarily located in Bermuda, where they enjoy tax benefits and are relatively free from regulation. The Islands, Guernsey, British Virgin Islands, Luxembourg and Barbados are also important centers for prisoners. Vermont is the main prison residence in the United States.

II. Self-insurance

Self-insurance can be purchased by individual companies that wish to retain risk, or by entities in similar industries or geographic locations that pool their resources to insure the risks of others. The use of higher deductibles/deductibles is on the rise in most insurance policies. In the area of employee benefits, many companies choose to maintain greater exposure through policies with high deductibles $100,000 or more. The major franchises, first introduced in 1989, now command a significant share of the market.

III. Third party risk retention groups

The Risk Retention Group (RRG) is a company owned and operated by its members. It must be incorporated and licensed as a liability insurance company under the laws of at least one state. The group can then purchase insurance in all other states. You do not need to obtain a license in any state other than the states you have authorized.

IV. Risk buying groups

Like risk retention groups (RRGs), buying groups must be composed of individuals or entities with similar exposures and in a joint venture. While RRGs are member-owned liability insurance companies, purchasing groups purchase liability coverage for their members from licensed insurers, excess lines, or RRGs. Some state laws prohibit insurers from allowing groups to purchase insurance benefits from individuals. However, buying groups are not subject to so-called "fictitious group" laws, which require the group to exist for a certain amount of time or to have a certain minimum number of members. The Retention of Risk Act of 1986 specifically mandated the establishment of buying groups to provide liability insurance for members of sponsoring groups.

V. **Catastrophe bonds and other alternative risk transfer products (ART)**

Several alternative risk transfer products (ARTs), such as insurance securities and time derivatives, have been developed to meet the financial risk transfer needs of companies. One such product, catastrophe (cat) bonds, risky securities sold in the capital markets, were developed after Hurricanes Andrew and Inky in 1992 and the 1994 Northridge earthquake, mega-disasters that caused a global reinsurance shortage. Insurance for insurers) for such accidents. Insurers authorized to use the capital market to diversify your risks and increase the number of insurance policies available in disaster prone areas. Zurich Financials Kamp Re was the first major catastrophe bond capitalized.

CHAPTER TWELVE

DISASTERS: INSURANCE ISSUES

The term **"catastrophe"** in the property insurance industry means a natural or man-made disaster of unusual severity. The industry calls a catastrophic event when claims are expected to reach a certain dollar threshold, currently set at $25 million, and more than a certain number of policyholders and insurance companies are affected.

The extent of the damage caused by Katrina and the potential damage that Hurricane Rita could have caused if it had not weakened into an intense Category 5 hurricane prompted re-examination, not only among insurers and reinsurers, but also among policymakers: how the United States is dealing with the financial consequences of such great material and personal damage.

Disaster losses along the coast are likely to increase in the coming years, in part due to the huge increase in development. A disaster modeling firm predicts that disaster losses will double roughly every decade due to increased residential and commercial density and more expensive buildings. Census Bureau data compiled by USA Today show that in 2006, 34.9 million people were at severe risk from Atlantic hurricanes, compared to 10.2 million in 1950. Prior to the 2005 hurricane season, Hurricane Andrew was listed as the only costliest natural disaster in the United States. Man-made disasters, such as the attacks on the World Trade Center, can also cause huge losses. The attacks prompted Congress to authorize the terrorist risk Insurance Act (TRIA) in November 2002. Since then, TRIA has been reauthorized twice. The most recent reauthorization, approved in late 2007, extends the law through 2014.

TRIA provides federal relief for commercial insurance losses caused by acts of terrorism, making it easier for insurers to calculate maximum losses. For such a disaster and how to secure cover, see Terrorism Risk and Insurance.

Typical home insurance covers damage from fire, storms, hail, riots and explosions, as well as other types of losses, such as theft and living expenses elsewhere, while the structure is repaired or rebuilt after damage. Commercial property insurance generally covers the same causes of loss with some variation depending on the coverage chosen. Flood and earthquake damage is excluded from the homeowner's policy (separate policies are available), but is covered by the extended portion of the standard auto policy, which is signed by more than 75% of drivers whose auto liability insurance is closed.

The insurance industry tracks catastrophes to track claims costs and assigns a number to each catastrophe. Each claim arising from the event is tagged so that total losses for the entire industry can be tabulated. The term catastrophe is often used in the property insurance industry to refer to a catastrophic event that exceeds a monetary threshold in claims payments.

This figure has changed over the years due to inflation and increased development in areas prone to natural disasters. Beginning in 1997, the definition of a catastrophe was changed from $5 million to $25 million in insured damages.

There were four disasters that fall into the category of mega disasters and are well above the $25 million threshold. The first two, Hurricane Andrew (1992) and the Northridge earthquake (1994), were watershed events because they were far more devastating than most experts predicted would be a disaster would be of this type. The third, the terrorist attack on the World Trade Center in 2001, changed the attitude of insurers towards man-made risks around the world.

Mobile Phones and Driving

Increased reliance on mobile phones has led to an increase in the number of people using these devices while driving. There are two dangers associated with driving and using cell phones, including texting. First, when marking, drivers must take their eyes off the road. Second, people can become so engrossed in their conversations that their ability to concentrate while driving is seriously impaired, putting the safety of passengers and pedestrians at risk. Since the first law passed in New York in 2001 prohibiting the use of cell phones during the ride there were discussions about the exact nature and degree of danger.

Recent research shows that cell phone use while driving may not be the most dangerous distraction, as it is so common that it is by far the most common distraction in crashes and accidents.

CHAPTER THIRTEEN

CLIMATE CHANGE: INSURANCE PROBLEMS

There is presently an agreement throughout the scientific community that the climate is changing, with possible threats to the world economy, ecosystem and people.

As risk bearers, insurers aim to limit possible losses every day via a process called risk management. Because climate change might inflict losses on an unprecedented scale, insurers are not waiting for experts to uncover all the answers.

Meanwhile, societal worries about climate change give insurers with new leadership possibilities and new chances for creative products.

Global warming: when fossil fuels (coal, oil and natural gas) are used to create energy, so-called greenhouse gases, chiefly carbon dioxide, are released into the atmosphere, where they trap heat. Forests and seas can absorb some carbon. But to avoid the most catastrophic effects of what is being predicted, researchers must drastically reduce carbon emissions, well seeking to reduce overall energy consumption, increase the use of energy from renewable sources such as solar heat, and limit the use of paper and other tree products that absorb carbon dioxide during the photosynthesis process.

Property losses of all types are expected to grow, and there is a possibility of much bigger corporate liability losses as shareholders and consumers attempt to hold firms responsible for changes in the environment.

Insurers' role to decreasing greenhouse gas emissions: Like corporations in other industries, insurers are advocating ways to decrease greenhouse gas emissions. Some insurers have been warning policymakers and the general public about the threat of climate change for years, and others are among the first to adopt public statements on the environment and climate change and join business coalitions calling on the federal government to enact legislation to reduce greenhouse gases. Some, notably reinsurers, support research and partner with others interested in the same sorts of solutions, such as discovering methods for individuals and society to adapt to harsh weather, especially in poor nations.

Many insurance firms have vowed to cut their own overall greenhouse gas emissions and offset the remaining via donations to reforestation and renewable energy initiatives. They also push their staff to embrace "green" measures in their private life. Some engaged in greenhouse gas reduction programs before such efforts garnered public notice, and many are now supporting their policyholders' desire to lessen their carbon footprint by providing paperless invoicing and paperwork. Some have increased the quality of company websites to attract policyholders to conduct business online. At least one vehicle insurance offers coverage completely online.

Insurers are also working on another front minimizing the frequency and expense of property damage caused by occurrences that are still occuring, despite society's attempts to minimize greenhouse gases.

New goods and commercial opportunities: Without insurance, the economy could not run. Insurers basically license new goods and services they are built with the risk of loss in mind. Just as they swiftly changed liability insurance from horse-drawn carriages or draft horses to vehicles in the late 1800s, they are now reacting to climate change efforts in the early 21st century.

There are possibilities on various fronts. First, there are new risks that need to be insured, including new sectors, such as wind farms and other alternative fuel installations, and new financial risks, such as those linked with carbon trading. Carbon trading insurance products safeguard investors who invest in clean technology initiatives against the project's inability to acquire approved allocations. Several firms also provide carbon project risk management consulting services to their customers. With a carbon credit, the owner is entitled to emit one ton of carbon. The Kyoto Protocol and other cap-and-trade systems now under debate put limits on carbon production and enable individuals who generate less than the limit to sell credits to those who exceed the limit. Investors in clean technology initiatives such as afforestation and renewable energy acquire credit rights and resale them on the worldwide carbon market.

Among the related risks with the acquisition of carbon trading rights is that the technology/project aimed to minimize carbon emissions will not meet expectations or the firm will go bankrupt before completing the contract, leaving the investor without reimbursement for the needed carbon.

Secondly, the need to prevent global warming has led the establishment of insurance plans that incentivize policyholders to contribute to these efforts. These include vehicle insurance reductions for having a hybrid car and driving with lower mileage and green building coverage.

Auto Insurance Initiatives: Motor vehicles are responsible for more than 25% of all greenhouse gas emissions in the United States. According to Ceres, a network of organizations devoted to global safety, insurance policies such as pay-per-drive, incorporating mileage in the price of insurance, and discounts on hybrid vehicles might cut that figure by more than 10% if broadly adopted worldwide warming. A Brookings Institute analysis finds that driving would reduce by 8% if drivers paid per mile.

There are two strategies to minimize the greenhouse gas emissions connected with driving. One is to encourage consumers to purchase automobiles that produce less carbon dioxide into the environment and have higher gas economy. Several firms provide discounts to customers who drive hybrid automobiles; Some think that socially conscious people are also more responsible behind the wheel. Another method is to compensate individuals for driving less miles, which is known as pay-per-drive (PAYD) vehicle insurance. Several insurers have devised technology-based discount schemes that give financial rewards for driving fewer miles. Mileage comes from a particular gadget. In some, it's attached to the car's speedometer, while in others it's a wireless sensor that can detect speed and distance. These programs are provided in a growing number of nations. Additionally, California and numerous other states are supporting the creation of PAYD systems.

Insurers assist encourage sustainable construction practices by providing green coverage for household and commercial property owners. In addition, they are responding to the increased need for aid in energy projects and carbon reductions with risk management services that address global warming.

Securing "green" buildings: Homeowners at the vanguard of the environmental sustainability movement are increasingly producing their own geothermal, solar or wind energy and selling surplus power to the local grid. Several insurers are breaking this trend by providing a house coverage that covers both loss of income and loss of power. Termination of the covered risk and extra expense for the owner associated to the purchase of power from another source. Policies frequently pay charges to come back online, such as utility bills for inspection and reconnection.

Some insurers provide homes insurance policies that, in the case of a fire or other tragedy, enable policyholders to rebuild to environmentally friendly "green" standards, even if they didn't acquire such a coverage in the first place. Green standards, which are part of the sustainable development movement, contain references to energy savings and the use of renewable construction materials. The Green Building Council introduced its Leadership in Energy and Environmental Design (LEED) accreditation program in 2001. According to Ceres, buildings are responsible for more than a third of greenhouse gas emissions, and green building measures may cut energy usage and emissions by more than 50 percent. As the development of green commercial buildings is likely to rise dramatically in the next years, an increasing number of insurers are providing green commercial property insurance and endorsements, some of which target particular parts of the corporate world, such as manufacturers.

Generally, the policy permits building owners to replace damaged facilities, whether certified green or not, with green alternatives, including energy-efficient electrical equipment and interior lighting, water-saving plumbing fixtures, and non-toxic paint and carpeting. They may also pay for HVAC system inspections, building recertification costs, green or vegetated roof replacements, and garbage recycling. Some compensate lost revenue and expenditures incurred when alternative power producing equipment is broken.

Earthquakes: Risk and Insurance Issues

An earthquake is a quick, fast shaking of the ground produced by the shattering and shifting of rocks under the earth's surface. These earthquakes may occasionally trigger landslides, avalanches, flash floods, fires and tsunamis.

Earthquakes in the United States are not covered by regular house or business insurance. Coverage is frequently offered for earthquake damage in the form of a house or business insurance policy. However, insurers who do not issue earthquake insurance may still be impacted by these catastrophes owing to post-shock fire losses. These losses may also include claims for company losses and increased living expenditures. Cars and other vehicles are covered for damages caused by earthquakes under the comprehensive component of the car insurance policy.

About 5,000 earthquakes occur in the United States each year. Earthquakes have occurred in 39 states since 1900 and have caused damage in all 50. One of the deadliest catastrophes in US history, the 1906 San Francisco earthquake is thought to have generated $96 billion in insurance damages. transpired under the existing settings. economic and demographic factors, according to AIR Worldwide. The potential costs of earthquakes have grown owing to rising urban expansion in seismically active regions and the fragility of older structures, which may not have been constructed or modified to current construction requirements.

The Northridge earthquake, which hit southern California on January 17, 1994, was the costliest earthquake in United States history, inflicting property damage estimated at $20 billion, including $12.5 billion in insurance claims. Subsequently, in 1996, the California Earthquake Authority (CEA) was founded. Fearing bankruptcy from another significant earthquake, the great majority of insurers in the state's house insurance market dramatically cut or terminated coverage following Northridge. To secure the availability of coverage for homeowners and address a severe danger to the health of the state's housing market, the California Legislature formed the CEA as a state-owned and primarily private-sector supported agency.

Only around 12% of Californians purchase earthquake data now, compared to roughly 30% in 1996, when the terrible 1994 Northridge earthquake was still fresh in people's memories. To entice more Californians to obtain coverage, the CEA authorized a 22% reduced average premium, commencing July 1, 2006. The CEA reports a dramatic drop in reinsurance prices and many years without a large earthquake, which might impair accrued reserves.

Losses from recent large earthquakes

Two big earthquakes occurred in early 2010: a magnitude 7.0 earthquake in Haiti in January and a magnitude 8.8 earthquake in Chile in February. The earthquake in Haiti killed more than 220,000 people and cost eight billion dollars in damage, most of which were uninsured. The earthquake in Chile, albeit stronger, was significantly less fatal because the epicenter was in a relatively sparsely populated zone and because Chile's history of terrible earthquakes has led to rigorous construction rules. The earthquake in Chile and the associated tsunami caused more than $4 billion in insured losses and more than $20 billion in total damages (including insured and uninsured losses), according to Munich Re. He murdered roughly 500 people.

Financial and Market Conditions

Many elements impact the price, availability and safety of insurance products. Some are external, such as the status of the economy, changes in interest rates and the stock market, regulatory action, the quantity and severity of natural catastrophes, the growth of litigation and increased compensation. Others are internal, such as the amount of competitiveness.

Fortunately, insurance businesses act carefully as though every day may bring a new calamity, so despite the present economic and financial situations, the sector has functioned as usual. contrary to banks and insurance companies have little debt (they generally do not raise loans for investment or settlement of claims); they limit the risk they take on to the available capital; and since they don't sell the risks they take elsewhere – they have some "skin in the game" – they have to underwrite carefully or suffer the consequences.

The insurance sector is cyclical. Rates and earnings change according on the point of the cycle, particularly with commercial hedges. The return cycle may vary somewhat for various forms of insurance.

The cycle of the early to mid-1980s was one of the worst the business had ever experienced. This cycle was centered on civil liability insurance. The most recent challenging market started in early 2001 and peaked in early 2004. The industry suffered a difficult market owing to the bad economy.

Insurance Cycle: The property/casualty insurance market has been cyclical for many years, going back to 1920. These cycles are defined by periods of increasing interest rates leading to increased profitability.

In a time of solid but unspectacular profits, the sector experiences a crisis in which prices fall, insurance supply becomes ample, and finally profitability decreases or vanishes completely. At the turn of the cycle, when profits decrease, the underlying capacity of insurance firms to take on new business or, for certain businesses, even to renew some current policies, might suffer as the capital required to maintain them is drained by losses. Cycles vary in difficulty.

The cycle in the insurance sector is no different from the cycle that happens in agriculture, for example in the wheat and meat markets. Demand for products in both sectors is relatively stable and relatively insensitive to price changes, while supply can vary from year to year. This means that when supply increases, a drop in price does not immediately "clean" the excess supply from the market. If the price of car insurance is cut in half, people will still buy only one policy, even though they may increase the amount of coverage they buy.

In the 1950s and 1960s, the cycles were regular, with a three-year soft rating period followed by a three-year hard rating for almost all types of accident/casualty insurance. There were only two cycles in the 1970s and 1980s, one that predominantly impacted vehicle insurance in the mid-1970s and another in the mid-1980s that affected business liability insurance. The cycle of commercial general liability insurance led to a "liability crisis", when it became impossible to get certain forms of commercial general liability coverage, such as insurance for childcare facilities, municipalities, ski resorts and any places that serve alcohol. Since then, with the exception of the difficulties of getting medical malpractice insurance at the beginning of the previous decade, the insurance cycle has had minimal influence on the public.

www.ingramcontent.com/pod-product-compliance
Lightning Source LLC
LaVergne TN
LVHW090414210926
848480LV00002B/565